Advanced Information Technology Assignments

SECOND EDITION

Rita Molland DipRSA FSBT AIQPS

LONGMAN

Addison Wesley Longman Limited
Edinburgh Gate, Harlow
Essex CM20 2JE, England
and Associated Companies throughout the world

First published in Great Britain 1991
Second Edition published 1995
Second impression published by Longman Group Limited 1995
Reprinted 1996

British Library Cataloguing in Publication Data
A catalogue entry for this title is available from the British Library.

ISBN 0-582-28876-2

Library of Congress Cataloging-in-Publication Data
A catalog entry for this title is available from the Library of Congress.

Printed in Singapore
by Longman Singapore Publishers Pte Ltd.

Contents

Acknowledgements

I would like to thank my friend and colleague Barbara Smith for her assistance in the compilation of the Theatre assignments.

I am also very grateful for the help (and constructive criticism!) of my students at Salisbury College (especially Richard) who struggled with the assignments! In passing their external examinations, they proved that practising the tasks in the book equipped them with the necessary knowledge and skills.

Introduction

This book provides practice material for students who wish to study for advanced Information Technology examinations. The object of such exams is to assess the candidate's ability to collect together a variety of Information Technology facilities to:

· analyse and select appropriate information
· construct a suitable framework for handling the information
· input and store data
· manipulate data
· sort data and present it in different ways.

Examinations for which the text is suitable include:

GNVQ - all levels
RSA IT II
ATT and IOB Preliminary
PEI Intermediate
LCCI.

The applications covered are Databases, Spreadsheets, Word Processing, Graphics and Collating. For each of these applications a set of source documents is provided. The student is required to appraise the material and extract and manipulate the relevant information in order to complete the assignment.

The **Database** tasks consist of approximately 30 records, each containing 6-8 fields. In order to make the assignments more realistic the records are presented in different formats, eg individual cards as if they have been completed by a clerk in an office, or possibly by a customer requesting or giving information, or sometimes in tabular form. The student is required to set up the database, enter the data and interrogate the data in order to produce selected print-outs.

Skills required:

· ability to choose relevant data and omit unrequired fields

· creation of suitable database framework to store the information

· ability to search on three criteria

The **Spreadsheet** sections are in the form of financial/numerical information, giving the relevant statistical data. The student is expected to decide upon a layout for the spreadsheet and may find it necessary to experiment with various formats before deciding upon the one which best suits the particular problem. The student will need to analyse the information given in order to produce a spreadsheet containing between 100 and 130 cells. Printing will include part only of the spreadsheet, and also the formulae. The student will also be expected to be able to produce results based on various "what-if" projections.

Skills required:

- manipulation of the given data
- "freezing" columns and rows
- calculation of percentages
- printing labels and a distant column/row of figures
- copying the original file so that duplicate copies can be worked on

For the **Word Processing** assignments, the student is presented with a draft, which may be a mixture of typescript and handwritten text, consisting of approximately 450 words.

Skills required:

- numbering of pages
- inclusion of a table
- leaving vertical space to given measurements
- following formatting instructions such as "embolden", "underline" and "double line spacing"

The **Graphics** section involves the student in producing a graphical representation of some part of the spreadsheet or other given figures. It is necessary to include a main heading (and possibly a sub-heading) together with X and Y axis labels, and print out the graph.

Collating requires the student to bring together the previous sections of the assignments, by integrating part of each one with the word processed document.

Solutions have been provided for each of the assignments. Printouts from different machines will obviously vary in their display, but the essential information will remain the same. Note that, especially in the spreadsheet section, there are several possible layouts, and no one layout is any more "correct" than any other.

The Assignments

There are six sets of assignments, each with a common theme relating to a business or leisure-time activity. In each case, the collating assignment brings all the sections together.

1. Little Theatre

The Database assignment consists of membership cards giving information on the individual, eg whether or not the member is a car owner, and which particular aspects of theatre interest them.

In the Spreadsheet assignment, the details refer to all the costs incurred in the last four productions. Some of the productions made a loss, and the projections required take into account the increased ticket price.

The Word Processing assignment is an information sheet to prospective members, discussing the progress of the club since its inception. The problems associated with the acquisition of its own premises are mentioned, and there is an analysis of the success/failure of the last four productions.

The Graphics section illustrates the range of members' skills.

2. Health and Fitness Club

The Database consists of enrolment cards for prospective members, detailing personal information and their particular interests.

The Management has constructed a rough Spreadsheet giving income and expenditure for the previous year, but needs to know how the situation would be altered if costs were increased.

The Word Processing assignment consists of a newsletter to existing and prospective members of the Club.

In the Graphics assignment students are required to illustrate a breakdown of current membership.

3. Publishing Company

In the Database you will dealing with details of books which have been published in the last few years.

Information for the Spreadsheet is taken from the Recent Publications List and the Sales figures. You will be calculating royalties due to the authors.

The Word Processing assignment takes the form of an annual newsletter which discusses royalties and highlights problems with sales of certain categories of books.

The Graphics assignment compares sales figures for a given year.

4. Horticultural Show

The Database contains profiles of plants which the Committee is considering for the competition.

Spreadsheet details include the number of entries in all classes, and the costs incurred in mounting a show. Projections are based on increased prices for the following year.

The Word Processing document is the chairperson's presentation of the schedule for a forthcoming show, including entertainments which have been arranged for the day.

The Graphics assignment shows the number of entries in the handicraft section.

5. College Courses

The Database assignment is concerned with personal details, course applied for, and examination achievements of students applying for courses.

The Spreadsheet explores the costs involved in providing leisure courses, and seeks projections based on increasing costs.

The Word Processing section discusses the courses offered by one department. It mentions equipment in use, and being acquired, and addresses the problem of the cost of setting up courses.

In the Graphics section the number of applications for various courses is illustrated.

6. Hotel Accommodation

An enterprising businessman has started a new company to provide information to organisations and individuals on the facilities available at hotels within a 25-mile radius of the town. The database assignment is the first attempt at collecting such information together.

The spreadsheet is a comparison of charges from three hotels for providing accommodation, etc, for a couple's wedding reception.

In the word processing assignment, the manager of a small chain of hotels is setting out the facilities which the chain is able to provide.

The graphics assignment illustrates comparative prices for wedding reception accommodation from three hotels.

1 *The Little Theatre*

Scenario

The Little Theatre - a well-known amateur dramatic society - has been in existence for the last ten years. Originally members joined as general assistants but more recently they have specialised in make-up, acting, production, catering, stage management, lighting, front-of-house and wardrobe.

Last year the society presented four plays - *Mother Courage, Anne Frank, See How They Run,* and *The Tempest.*

Next week, the Annual General Meeting and a New Production Committee Meeting appear on the society's calendar. As a general assistant, you have been asked by the chairperson to perform the following tasks:

Task 1 Database

Create the latest recruitment disk and from it obtain specific personal details in order that the New Production Committee can decide on the next play to be presented.

Task 2 Spreadsheet

Produce a financial breakdown of last year's productions - both for the AGM and the Committee.

Task 3 Word Processing

Start to compile the Chairperson's Report for photocopying and distribution at the AGM.

Task 4 Graphics

Produce a breakdown of current members' skills for the Chairperson's Report.

Task 5 Collating

Complete the Chairperson's Report by inserting the graphics and extracting the required information from the recruitment disk and financial breakdown of last year's productions.

Database Assignment (solutions pages 89-90)

Membership

1 Refer to the "Little Theatre" membership cards and create a database with each record containing the following information:

Surname, forename and sex

Special interest (use a two-letter code)

MU = makeup
AC = acting
PR = production
CA = catering
SM = stage management
FH = front of house
LI = lighting
GN = general

Area of preference (use a one-letter code)

S = Shakespeare
C = comedy
D = drama
M = mystery

Telephone number

Car owner or not

2 Save the information.

3 Print the following lists (if possible include a heading for each column):

a The whole file in alphabetical order of surname;

b Names and telephone numbers of females whose preference is Shakespearean productions:

c All the information on males whose special interest is described as "Front of House";

d Names and telephone numbers of anyone interested in Stage Management - include on the printout whether male or female:

e Names of those people who wish to act in a comedy;

f All the information for those people who own cars and have said they are willing to help with production or stage management.

THE LITTLE THEATRE MEMBERSHIP APPLICATION			
SURNAME: Little			SEX: M/F F
FORENAME: Frances			TEL NO: 8832
ADDRESS: 2, The Park, Bath, Avon. BA2 9HR.			CAR OWNER? YES/NO Yes
SPECIAL INTEREST:		PREFERENCE:	
Make-up	YES/NO No	Shakespeare	YES/NO No
Acting	YES/NO No	Comedy	YES/NO Yes
Production	YES/NO No	Drama	YES/NO No
Catering	YES/NO No	Mystery	YES/NO No
Stage Management	YES/NO Yes	Other	YES/NO No
Front of House	YES/NO No	For office use only:	
Lighting	YES/NO No	Membership fee	
General	YES/NO No	Card issued	

THE LITTLE THEATRE MEMBERSHIP APPLICATION			
SURNAME: ADAMS			SEX: M/F F.
FORENAME: MONICA			TEL NO:
ADDRESS: The Bolt Hole, Fenny Avenue, Puckeridge.			CAR OWNER? YES/NO NO
SPECIAL INTEREST:		PREFERENCE:	
Make-up	YES/NO YES	Shakespeare	YES/NO (NO circled)
Acting	YES/NO (NO circled)	Comedy	YES/NO YES
Production	YES/NO (NO circled)	Drama	YES/NO (NO circled)
Catering	YES/NO (NO circled)	Mystery	YES/NO (NO circled)
Stage Management	YES/NO (NO circled)	Other	YES/NO (NO circled)
Front of House	YES/NO (NO circled)	For office use only:	
Lighting	YES/NO (NO circled)	Membership fee	
General	YES/NO (NO circled)	Card issued	

THE LITTLE THEATRE
MEMBERSHIP APPLICATION

SURNAME: JONES	SEX: M/F (M circled)
FORENAME: Ray	TEL NO: 39210
ADDRESS: 42, The Ridgeway, Radlett, Herts. 3HB 760	CAR OWNER? YES/NO (NO circled)

SPECIAL INTEREST:		PREFERENCE:	
Make-up	YES/NO No	Shakespeare	YES/NO No
Acting	YES/NO No	Comedy	YES/NO No
Production	YES/NO No	Drama	YES/NO YES
Catering	YES/NO Yes	Mystery	YES/NO No
Stage Management	YES/NO No	Other	YES/NO No
Front of House	YES/NO No	For office use only:	
Lighting	YES/NO No	Membership fee	
General	YES/NO No	Card issued	

THE LITTLE THEATRE
MEMBERSHIP APPLICATION

SURNAME: Friend	SEX: M/F m.
FORENAME: Alan	TEL NO: Ex-dir.
ADDRESS: 19, Hill View, Midsomer Norton.	CAR OWNER? YES/NO yes.

SPECIAL INTEREST:		PREFERENCE:	
Make-up	YES/NO no	Shakespeare	YES/NO yes
Acting	YES/NO yes	Comedy	YES/NO no
Production	YES/NO no	Drama	YES/NO no
Catering	YES/NO no	Mystery	YES/NO no
Stage Management	YES/NO no	Other	YES/NO no
Front of House	YES/NO no	For office use only:	
Lighting	YES/NO no	Membership fee	
General	YES/NO no	Card issued	

THE LITTLE THEATRE
MEMBERSHIP APPLICATION

SURNAME: ~~John~~ Jennings	SEX: (M)/F
FORENAME: John	TEL NO: 339712
ADDRESS: 102, Rainbow Road, Bradford-on-Avon. BR3 179	CAR OWNER? (YES)/NO

SPECIAL INTEREST:		PREFERENCE:	
Make-up	(YES)/NO	Shakespeare	YES/(NO)
Acting	YES/(NO)	Comedy	YES/(NO)
Production	YES/(NO)	Drama	YES/(NO)
Catering	YES/(NO)	Mystery	(YES)/NO
Stage Management	YES/(NO)	Other	YES/(NO)
Front of House	YES/(NO)	For office use only:	
Lighting	YES/(NO)	Membership fee	
General	YES/(NO)	Card issued	

THE LITTLE THEATRE
MEMBERSHIP APPLICATION

SURNAME: Britain	SEX: M/F F.
FORENAME: Beryl	TEL NO: 23711
ADDRESS: 3, The Royal Crescent, Bath.	CAR OWNER? YES/NO NO

SPECIAL INTEREST:		PREFERENCE:	
Make-up	YES/NO N	Shakespeare	YES/NO N
Acting	YES/NO N	Comedy	YES/NO Y
Production	YES/NO Y	Drama	YES/NO N
Catering	YES/NO N	Mystery	YES/NO N
Stage Management	YES/NO N	Other	YES/NO N
Front of House	YES/NO N	For office use only:	
Lighting	YES/NO N	Membership fee	
General	YES/NO N	Card issued	

THE LITTLE THEATRE
MEMBERSHIP APPLICATION

SURNAME: Coombs.	SEX: M/F (M circled)
FORENAME: Andrew	TEL NO: 21484
ADDRESS: 81, Upper Oldfield Park, Bath, Avon.	CAR OWNER? YES/NO (YES circled)

SPECIAL INTEREST:		PREFERENCE:	
Make-up	YES/NO N	Shakespeare	YES/NO N
Acting	YES/NO N	Comedy	YES/NO N
Production	YES/NO N	Drama	YES/NO N
Catering	YES/NO N	Mystery	YES/NO Yes
Stage Management	YES/NO N	Other	YES/NO N
Front of House	YES/NO N	For office use only:	
Lighting	YES/NO N	Membership fee	
General	YES/NO Yes	Card issued	

THE LITTLE THEATRE
MEMBERSHIP APPLICATION

SURNAME: Gaspard	SEX: M/F (M circled)
FORENAME: René	TEL NO: 60603
ADDRESS: 9, The Laurels, Frenchay, Bristol.	CAR OWNER? YES/NO (YES circled)

SPECIAL INTEREST:		PREFERENCE:	
Make-up	YES/NO	Shakespeare	YES/NO
Acting	YES/NO	Comedy	YES/NO
Production	YES/NO	Drama	YES/NO Yes
Catering	YES/NO	Mystery	YES/NO
Stage Management	YES/NO Yes	Other	YES/NO
Front of House	YES/NO	For office use only:	
Lighting	YES/NO	Membership fee	
General	YES/NO	Card issued	

THE LITTLE THEATRE MEMBERSHIP APPLICATION	
SURNAME: Bertram	SEX: M/F F
FORENAME: Adele	TEL NO: 23611
ADDRESS: 17, Peacock St., Puckeridge, Avon.	CAR OWNER? YES/NO No

SPECIAL INTEREST:		PREFERENCE:	
Make-up	YES/NO	Shakespeare	YES/NO ✓
Acting	YES/NO	Comedy	YES/NO
Production	YES/NO	Drama	YES/NO
Catering	YES/NO	Mystery	YES/NO
Stage Management	YES/NO	Other	YES/NO
Front of House	YES/NO	For office use only:	
Lighting	YES/NO ✓	Membership fee	
General	YES/NO	Card issued	

THE LITTLE THEATRE MEMBERSHIP APPLICATION	
SURNAME: TALESMAN	SEX: M/F F.
FORENAME: CAROLE	TEL NO: 55560
ADDRESS: 94, WAGGONERS WAY, KEYNSHAM, NR. BRISTOL.	CAR OWNER? YES/NO YES

SPECIAL INTEREST:		PREFERENCE:	
Make-up	YES/NO	Shakespeare	YES/NO Y.
Acting	YES/NO	Comedy	YES/NO
Production	YES/NO	Drama	YES/NO
Catering	YES/NO	Mystery	YES/NO
Stage Management	YES/NO	Other	YES/NO
Front of House	YES/NO Y.	For office use only:	
Lighting	YES/NO	Membership fee	
General	YES/NO	Card issued	

THE LITTLE THEATRE MEMBERSHIP APPLICATION			
SURNAME: VARCOE		SEX: M/F F.	
FORENAME: SHEILA		TEL NO: 6811	
ADDRESS: THE OLD RECTORY, COOMBE DOWN, AVON.		CAR OWNER? YES/NO YES	
SPECIAL INTEREST:		PREFERENCE:	
Make-up	YES/NO YES	Shakespeare	YES/NO NO
Acting	YES/NO NO	Comedy	YES/NO NO
Production	YES/NO NO	Drama	YES/NO YES
Catering	YES/NO NO	Mystery	YES/NO NO
Stage Management	YES/NO NO	Other	YES/NO NO
Front of House	YES/NO NO	For office use only:	
Lighting	YES/NO NO	Membership fee	
General	YES/NO NO	Card issued	

THE LITTLE THEATRE MEMBERSHIP APPLICATION			
SURNAME: Smithson		SEX: M/F F.	
FORENAME: Jeannie		TEL NO: 268 115	
ADDRESS: 41, Broughan Hayes, Bath, Avon.		CAR OWNER? YES/NO	
SPECIAL INTEREST:		PREFERENCE:	
Make-up	YES/NO —	Shakespeare	YES/NO ~~Yes~~ —
Acting	YES/NO —	Comedy	YES/NO —
Production	YES/NO Yes	Drama	YES/NO Yes
Catering	YES/NO —	Mystery	YES/NO —
Stage Management	YES/NO —	Other	YES/NO —
Front of House	YES/NO —	For office use only:	
Lighting	YES/NO —	Membership fee	
General	YES/NO —	Card issued	

THE LITTLE THEATRE MEMBERSHIP APPLICATION			
SURNAME: FROOL			SEX: M/F m
FORENAME: raymond			TEL NO: 3336
ADDRESS: 7, PEAR ~~AVENEX~~ AVE. WELLS			CAR OWNER? YES/NO NO
SPECIAL INTEREST:		PREFERENCE:	
Make-up	YES/NO	Shakespeare	YES/NO
Acting	YES/NO	Comedy	YES/NO
Production	YES/NO	Drama	YES/NO ✓
Catering	YES/NO	Mystery	YES/NO
Stage Management	YES/NO	Other	YES/NO
Front of House	YES/NO ✓	For office use only:	
Lighting	YES/NO	Membership fee	
General	YES/NO	Card issued	

THE LITTLE THEATRE MEMBERSHIP APPLICATION			
SURNAME: Gregory			SEX: M/F
FORENAME: Lance			TEL NO: –
ADDRESS: 66, Nelson Street, Midsommer Norton.			CAR OWNER? YES/NO
SPECIAL INTEREST:		PREFERENCE:	
Make-up	YES/NO	Shakespeare	YES/NO
Acting	YES/NO	Comedy	YES/NO
Production	YES/NO	Drama	YES/NO
Catering	YES/NO	Mystery	YES/NO
Stage Management	YES/NO	Other	YES/NO
Front of House	YES/NO	For office use only:	
Lighting	YES/NO	Membership fee	
General	YES/NO	Card issued	

THE LITTLE THEATRE
MEMBERSHIP APPLICATION

SURNAME: ROBBINS	SEX: M/F (M circled)
FORENAME: Matthew	TEL NO: 21088
ADDRESS: 4, Spring St., Bristol.	CAR OWNER? YES/NO (NO circled)

SPECIAL INTEREST:		PREFERENCE:	
Make-up	YES/NO –	Shakespeare	YES/NO YES
Acting	YES/NO –	Comedy	YES/NO –
Production	YES/NO –	Drama	YES/NO –
Catering	YES/NO –	Mystery	YES/NO –
Stage Management	YES/NO –	Other	YES/NO –
Front of House	YES/NO –	For office use only:	
Lighting	YES/NO –	Membership fee	
General	YES/NO YES.	Card issued	

THE LITTLE THEATRE
MEMBERSHIP APPLICATION

SURNAME: ROBBINS	SEX: M/F (M circled)
FORENAME: Philip.	TEL NO: 21088
ADDRESS: 4, Spring St., Bristol	CAR OWNER? YES/NO (NO circled)

SPECIAL INTEREST:		PREFERENCE:	
Make-up	YES/NO –	Shakespeare	YES/NO ✓
Acting	YES/NO –	Comedy	YES/NO –
Production	YES/NO –	Drama	YES/NO –
Catering	YES/NO –	Mystery	YES/NO –
Stage Management	YES/NO –	Other	YES/NO –
Front of House	YES/NO –	For office use only:	
Lighting	YES/NO –	Membership fee	
General	YES/NO ✓	Card issued	

THE LITTLE THEATRE MEMBERSHIP APPLICATION	
SURNAME: KITCHENER	SEX: M/F F.
FORENAME: KATE	TEL NO: 66663
ADDRESS: THE MILLHOUSE, WHITEWAYS, BATH, AVON.	CAR OWNER? YES/NO No.

SPECIAL INTEREST:		PREFERENCE:	
Make-up	YES/NO YES	Shakespeare	YES/NO N.
Acting	YES/NO N.	Comedy	YES/NO YES.
Production	YES/NO N.	Drama	YES/NO N.
Catering	YES/NO N.	Mystery	YES/NO N.
Stage Management	YES/NO N.	Other	YES/NO N.
Front of House	YES/NO N.	For office use only:	
Lighting	YES/NO N.	Membership fee	
General	YES/NO N.	Card issued	

THE LITTLE THEATRE MEMBERSHIP APPLICATION	
SURNAME: Fosdike	SEX: M/F M.
FORENAME: Bert.	TEL NO: 99932.
ADDRESS: Dunroamin, Maple Terrace, Bristol.	CAR OWNER? YES/NO (YES circled)

SPECIAL INTEREST:		PREFERENCE:	
Make-up	YES/NO n	Shakespeare	YES/NO n
Acting	YES/NO (YES circled)	Comedy	YES/NO (YES circled)
Production	YES/NO n	Drama	YES/NO n
Catering	YES/NO n	Mystery	YES/NO n
Stage Management	YES/NO n	Other	YES/NO n
Front of House	YES/NO n	For office use only:	
Lighting	YES/NO n	Membership fee	
General	YES/NO n	Card issued	

THE LITTLE THEATRE
MEMBERSHIP APPLICATION

SURNAME: Acland	SEX: M/F
FORENAME: Hilary	TEL NO: 57891
ADDRESS: The Manor, Filton, Bristol.	CAR OWNER? YES/NO

SPECIAL INTEREST:		PREFERENCE:	
Make-up	YES/NO	Shakespeare	YES/NO
Acting	YES/NO	Comedy	YES/NO
Production	YES/NO	Drama	YES/NO
Catering	YES/NO	Mystery	YES/NO
Stage Management	YES/NO	Other	YES/NO
Front of House	YES/NO	For office use only:	
Lighting	YES/NO	Membership fee	
General	YES/NO	Card issued	

THE LITTLE THEATRE
MEMBERSHIP APPLICATION

SURNAME: GOLDING	SEX: M/F
FORENAME: MARTIN	TEL NO: 3610
ADDRESS: 72 BEECH CLOSE, PUCKERIDGE, AVON	CAR OWNER? YES/NO

SPECIAL INTEREST:		PREFERENCE:	
Make-up	YES/NO	Shakespeare	YES/NO
Acting	YES/NO	Comedy	YES/NO
Production	YES/NO	Drama	YES/NO
Catering	YES/NO	Mystery	YES/NO
Stage Management	YES/NO	Other	YES/NO
Front of House	YES/NO	For office use only:	
Lighting	YES/NO	Membership fee	
General	YES/NO	Card issued	

THE LITTLE THEATRE
MEMBERSHIP APPLICATION

SURNAME: Woodward	SEX: M/F M.
FORENAME: Edwin	TEL NO: 5560
ADDRESS: 2A, Brown Street, Bath, ZA4 931	CAR OWNER? YES/NO (YES circled)

SPECIAL INTEREST:		PREFERENCE:	
Make-up	YES/NO	Shakespeare	YES/NO Y
Acting	YES/NO Y	Comedy	YES/NO
Production	YES/NO	Drama	YES/NO
Catering	YES/NO	Mystery	YES/NO
Stage Management	YES/NO	Other	YES/NO
Front of House	YES/NO	For office use only:	
Lighting	YES/NO	Membership fee	
General	YES/NO	Card issued	

THE LITTLE THEATRE
MEMBERSHIP APPLICATION

SURNAME: Martin	SEX: M/F F.
FORENAME: Margaret	TEL NO: 44812
ADDRESS: Basement Flat, 91, The Terrace, Bristol.	CAR OWNER? YES/NO NO

SPECIAL INTEREST:		PREFERENCE:	
Make-up	YES/NO	Shakespeare	YES/NO
Acting	YES/NO	Comedy	YES/NO
Production	YES/NO ✓	Drama	YES/NO ✓
Catering	YES/NO	Mystery	YES/NO
Stage Management	YES/NO	Other	YES/NO
Front of House	YES/NO	For office use only:	
Lighting	YES/NO	Membership fee	
General	YES/NO	Card issued	

THE LITTLE THEATRE
MEMBERSHIP APPLICATION

SURNAME: BELLINGER.	SEX: M/F (M circled)
FORENAME: Bernard.	TEL NO: 6630
ADDRESS: 76, Tower St., Keynsham. ~~YE~~ KE747 392	CAR OWNER? YES/NO (YES circled)

SPECIAL INTEREST:		PREFERENCE:	
Make-up	YES/NO –	Shakespeare	YES/NO –
Acting	YES/NO Yes	Comedy	YES/NO Yes
Production	YES/NO –	Drama	YES/NO –
Catering	YES/NO –	Mystery	YES/NO –
Stage Management	YES/NO –	Other	YES/NO –
Front of House	YES/NO –	For office use only:	
Lighting	YES/NO –	Membership fee	
General	YES/NO –	Card issued	

THE LITTLE THEATRE
MEMBERSHIP APPLICATION

SURNAME: MARTIN	SEX: M/F F.
FORENAME: JANET.	TEL NO: None
ADDRESS: 81, STRAIGHT STREET, (C/O MRS. McGILLICUDDY) BATH.	CAR OWNER? YES/NO YES.

SPECIAL INTEREST:		PREFERENCE:	
Make-up	YES/NO	Shakespeare	YES/NO ✓
Acting	YES/NO ✓	Comedy	YES/NO
Production	YES/NO	Drama	YES/NO
Catering	YES/NO	Mystery	YES/NO
Stage Management	YES/NO	Other	YES/NO
Front of House	YES/NO	For office use only:	
Lighting	YES/NO	Membership fee	
General	YES/NO	Card issued	

THE LITTLE THEATRE
MEMBERSHIP APPLICATION

SURNAME: Yoggi	SEX: M/F (M circled)
FORENAME: Max	TEL NO: 6444
ADDRESS: The New Garage, Frenchay, Bristol.	CAR OWNER? YES/NO (NO circled)

SPECIAL INTEREST:		PREFERENCE:	
Make-up	YES/NO	Shakespeare ✓	YES/NO
Acting	YES/NO	Comedy	YES/NO
Production	YES/NO	Drama	YES/NO
Catering	YES/NO	Mystery	YES/NO
Stage Management	YES/NO	Other	YES/NO
Front of House ✓	YES/NO	For office use only:	
Lighting	YES/NO	Membership fee	
General	YES/NO	Card issued	

THE LITTLE THEATRE
MEMBERSHIP APPLICATION

SURNAME: GRANT	SEX: M/F F.
FORENAME: Freda	TEL NO: 63029
ADDRESS: 110, SALT STREET, HARDWAYS, BATH.	CAR OWNER? YES/NO Y.

SPECIAL INTEREST:		PREFERENCE:	
Make-up	YES/NO Yes	Shakespeare	YES/NO No
Acting	YES/NO No	Comedy	YES/NO No
Production	YES/NO No	Drama	YES/NO Yes
Catering	YES/NO No	Mystery	YES/NO No
Stage Management	YES/NO No	Other	YES/NO No.
Front of House	YES/NO No	For office use only:	
Lighting	YES/NO No	Membership fee	
General	YES/NO No	Card issued	

THE LITTLE THEATRE MEMBERSHIP APPLICATION			
SURNAME: Churchman		SEX: M/F	
FORENAME: Charles		TEL NO: 9506	
ADDRESS: Palace House, The Old Walk, Wells.		CAR OWNER? YES/NO	
SPECIAL INTEREST:		PREFERENCE:	
Make-up	YES/NO	Shakespeare	YES/NO
Acting	YES/NO	Comedy	YES/NO
Production	YES/NO	Drama	YES/NO
Catering	YES/NO	Mystery	YES/NO
Stage Management	YES/NO	Other	YES/NO
Front of House	YES/NO	For office use only:	
Lighting	YES/NO	Membership fee	
General	YES/NO	Card issued	

THE LITTLE THEATRE MEMBERSHIP APPLICATION			
SURNAME: Prince.		SEX: M/F M.	
FORENAME: Christopher		TEL NO: 9 8711	
ADDRESS: 84a, Bruin Street, Keynsham.		CAR OWNER? YES/NO Y.	
SPECIAL INTEREST:		PREFERENCE:	
Make-up	YES/NO	Shakespeare	YES/NO
Acting	YES/NO ✓	Comedy	YES/NO
Production	YES/NO	Drama	YES/NO
Catering	YES/NO	Mystery	YES/NO ✓
Stage Management	YES/NO	Other	YES/NO
Front of House	YES/NO	For office use only:	
Lighting	YES/NO	Membership fee	
General	YES/NO	Card issued	

THE LITTLE THEATRE
MEMBERSHIP APPLICATION

SURNAME: Thomas	SEX: M/F (F circled)
FORENAME: Jill	TEL NO: 32019
ADDRESS: Wren Cottage, 3, Bismark Rd., Norton Radstock.	CAR OWNER? YES/NO (YES circled)

SPECIAL INTEREST:		PREFERENCE:	
Make-up	YES/NO	Shakespeare	YES/NO
Acting	YES/NO	Comedy (circled)	YES/NO
Production (circled)	YES/NO	Drama	YES/NO
Catering	YES/NO	Mystery	YES/NO
Stage Management	YES/NO	Other	YES/NO
Front of House	YES/NO	For office use only:	
Lighting	YES/NO	Membership fee	
General	YES/NO	Card issued	

THE LITTLE THEATRE
MEMBERSHIP APPLICATION

SURNAME: ROYAL	SEX: M/F M.
FORENAME: BERNARD.	TEL NO: 8772
ADDRESS: WIMBORNE MANOR, HINTON CHARTERHOUSE, AVON.	CAR OWNER? YES/NO NO

SPECIAL INTEREST:		PREFERENCE:	
Make-up	YES/NO N	Shakespeare	YES/NO ✓
Acting	YES/NO N	Comedy	YES/NO N
Production	YES/NO N	Drama	YES/NO N
Catering	YES/NO N	Mystery	YES/NO N
Stage Management	YES/NO N	Other	YES/NO N
Front of House	YES/NO ✓	For office use only:	
Lighting	YES/NO N	Membership fee	
General	YES/NO N	Card issued	

THE LITTLE THEATRE
MEMBERSHIP APPLICATION

SURNAME: SPUMANTI	SEX: M/F
FORENAME: CARMEN	TEL NO: Ex-Dir
ADDRESS: 15 Lower Birchwood Drive Bath	CAR OWNER? YES/NO

SPECIAL INTEREST:		PREFERENCE:	
Make-up	YES/NO	Shakespeare	YES/NO
Acting	YES/NO	Comedy	YES/NO
Production	YES/NO	Drama	YES/NO
Catering	YES/NO	Mystery	YES/NO
Stage Management	YES/NO	Other	YES/NO
Front of House	YES/NO	For office use only:	
Lighting	YES/NO	Membership fee	
General	YES/NO	Card issued	

THE LITTLE THEATRE
MEMBERSHIP APPLICATION

SURNAME: FOGARTY	SEX: M/F
FORENAME: Maxine	TEL NO: 36428
ADDRESS:	CAR OWNER? YES/NO ✓

SPECIAL INTEREST:		PREFERENCE:	
Make-up	YES/NO	Shakespeare	YES/NO
Acting	YES/NO	Comedy	YES/NO
Production	YES/NO	Drama	YES/NO
Catering	YES/NO	Mystery	YES/NO ✓
Stage Management	YES/NO ✓	Other	YES/NO
Front of House	YES/NO	For office use only:	
Lighting	YES/NO	Membership fee	
General	YES/NO	Card issued	

THE LITTLE THEATRE MEMBERSHIP APPLICATION			
SURNAME: PRITCHARD		SEX: M/F F.	
FORENAME: KAREN		TEL NO: 4482	
ADDRESS: 99, THE HILL, RIDGEWAY WILTS. R17 2BA		CAR OWNER? YES/NO No	
SPECIAL INTEREST:		PREFERENCE:	
Make-up	~~YES~~/NO	Shakespeare	~~YES~~/NO
Acting	~~YES~~/NO	Comedy	YES/~~NO~~
Production	~~YES~~/NO	Drama	~~YES~~/NO
Catering	YES/~~NO~~	Mystery	~~YES~~/NO
Stage Management	~~YES~~/NO	Other	~~YES~~/NO
Front of House	~~YES~~/NO	For office use only:	
Lighting	~~YES~~/NO	Membership fee	
General	~~YES~~/NO	Card issued	

Spreadsheet Assignment (solutions pages 91-94)

Production information

1 Using the following production statistics, construct a spreadsheet, and give it the title Production Statistics.

You should display the figures in two sections, Income and Expenses. The Income section should incorporate the seat cost and the number of seats sold for each production. Also include income derived from bar and programme sales. You will need a total of income from all sources.

The Expenses section must include all the costs and a total.

You are required to produce a final figure for Profit/Loss for each production.

2 Enter the data.

3 Please leave a few lines after the spreadsheet and insert the following information for the benefit of members, and calculate the totals.

	Adults	*Children*	*Total*
Stage Management	3	0	
Production	2	0	
Acting	34	15	
Scenery	25	3	
Front of House	15	0	
Box Office	5	0	
Refreshments	0	6	

4 Save and print two copies of the spreadsheet, one showing the figures and the other the formulae.

5 Insert an extra row in the Expenses section, and include an item for scripts of £15.58 per production. Adjust the data accordingly. Print out an amended spreadsheet.

6 We wish to know what difference it would have made if we had charged the same for all productions, ie £2.75. Please amend the appropriate figures and print out the whole spreadsheet again.

Production statistics

Four plays were produced this year:

Production 1 *Mother Courage*
Production 2 *Anne Frank*
Production 3 *See How They Run*
Production 4 The Tempest

Income

Seat Prices for Mother Courage and the Tempest were £2.50 each, and for the other two plays, £2.75.

The total number of seats sold for each production is as follows:

Mother Courage	70
Anne Frank	120
See How They Run	200
The Tempest	95

Other income was derived from bar takings and programme sales as follows:

	Bar	*Programmes*
	£	*£*
Mother Courage	40.56	7.00
Anne Frank	135.00	9.50
See How They Run	350.96	19.60
The Tempest	38.44	20.40

Expenses

Printing and advertising cost £35.00 for *Mother Courage*, and rose 2.5% for each subsequent production.

Heating and lighting averaged £30.00 per production.

Bar costs averaged £45.38 per production.

Props cost £34.75 for *Mother Courage* and £56.00 for *The Tempest* but none were purchased for the other plays.

Royalties average £70.00 for all plays except *The Tempest*, for which royalties are not now requested.

	£	
Costumes cost	12.75	for *Mother Courage*
	25.50	for *Anne Frank*
	224.12	for *See How They Run*
	156.80	for *The Tempest*

Word Processing Assignment (solution pages 95-96)

Chairperson's Report

1 **Create a file using single line spacing and justified right-hand margin.**

2 **Enter the following text and number the pages.**

3 **Save and print one copy.**

The Little Theatre ← Spaced Caps, Bold & centre

The Little Theatre was started ten years ago and has gone from strength to strength. We aim to stage a ~~mixture~~ variety of productions including comedy, tragedy, farce, musicals, ~~revues~~ revues and pantomime.

~~We~~ We have ~~been very~~ extremely fortunate in the past year to have obtained our own premises – and what ~~has~~ a difference it makes! Instead of having to transport scenery, lighting, costumes, etc, everything is located in one place. Absolute luxury, and we are still revelling in it!

Double spacing – add bold please

Of course, there have been problems associated with the acquisition, the main one being finance. The hall we have purchased ~~,~~ (or, to be more accurate, are purchasing ~~,~~ with a mortgage) cost £5,000, of which we were able to put £2,000 as a deposit, which leaves us still with a considerable amount to find. However, with determination and hard work, we are confident that we can repay the loan within the next ~~six~~ five years.

~~THE PLAY~~
THE PLAYS – Heading at margin Caps & underlined

This year, we have staged the following productions:

Mother Courage   See How They Run
Anne Frank   The Tempest

Two made a loss, one a slight profit, & the other a gratifyingly large profit. This is very encouraging, but we must not "rest on our laurels" – rather the opposite – and ~~we~~ ~~must~~ must go forward determined to do even better.

When we look for reasons to explain the losses made on the ~~first~~ two productions, it is obvious that we did not sell enough tickets, and members are urged to maintain their efforts to ~~publ~~ publicise productions and sell as many tickets as possible. Please do your best – remember, we depend on ticket sales as our main source of income.

Leave 1" here

When members first join, we do, of course, like to find out their own particular interest, whether it be acting, front of house, scenery painting, lighting etc. However, when a play is in production, everyone is ~~expected~~ (& is usually ~~very~~ very willing) to turn a hand to anything. (N.P.) // Thus we have the situation, as we did recently, where one of our members was ably taking the lead in "Mother Courage", but in the next production was in charge of interval refreshments. This way we find makes for good feeling and a sense of ~~comradeship, because it means that everyone is covering the whole range of activities & specialities available~~

fairness, all round.

SKILLS Heading at margin (Caps & underlined)

At any one time there are a number of people who could can be called upon to help in all sections - but as the following graph shows, clearly, the numbers offering to help with Stage Management and Production are very low.

leave 2" here

A PLEA Heading at margin caps & underlined

These jobs are a little more specialised, of course, but we would be very pleased if all members could give the matter some careful consideration. If you would be willing to help with any of these jobs perhaps you would like to contact one of the following, who will arrange for you to work alongside him/her learning the intricacies of the job.

Graphics Assignment (solution page 97)

Members' Skills

1 Using the additional details regarding members' skills which you included at the foot of your spreadsheet, create and label a chart showing the totals for each category.

Insert a main title: Members' Skills.

Label the x-axis with suitable abbreviations, and leave the y-axis unlabelled.

2 Save the display.

3 Print the display.

Collating Assignment (solution pages 98-100)

Chairperson's Report

1 Using the document produced in the word processing assignment, add the following to the text:

a From the graphics:

Include your graphical representation after the paragraph headed "Skills" or attach a copy of the diagram to the end of the document, as Appendix A, with *an appropriate note in the text.*

* b From the database :

At the end of the text insert the full names, interests and telephone numbers of those with cars who are willing to help with production or stage management.

* c From the spreadsheet:

After the paragraph which begins "When we look for reasons . . ." insert details of the income of seat sales for all four productions. Include relevant labels.

2 If necessary repaginate and renumber the pages.

3 Present the final document.

Note * These items must *not be re-keyed,* but should be included by:

a using integrated software to collate the different sections;

b printing out the extracts separately from the word processed document and then sticking them in at the appropriate places; OR

c using desktop publishing facilities.

2 *Health and Fitness Club*

Scenario

The Health and Fitness Club started business last year, offering a variety of facilities to its clients. Unfortunately a few months ago a fire destroyed its office and part of the main building.

The Club has recently re-opened, and now offers greatly improved recreational amenities, together with riverside bar and restaurant. It is also hoping to incorporate a swimming pool in the future.

You have just been taken on as an assistant in the newly furnished office, and have been asked by the Management to help the smooth running of the Club, by carrying out the following tasks.

Task 1 Database

Most of the clients' details were saved from the fire, but you are required to create a database of a few records which were damaged. You will need to search for incomplete records so that members can be asked to supply the missing information.

Task 2 Spreadsheet

Nearly all the financial records were destroyed, but the Manager has managed to collect some figures together. You are required to set up a spreadsheet using these figures in order that some predictions about the Club's future can be made.

Task 3 Word Processing

The Manager has drafted a newsletter for general distribution. You are required to produce a neat copy of this so that it can be checked, amended if necessary, and sent to the printers.

Task 4 Graphics

You are to produce a chart showing the current membership, for inclusion in the newsletter.

Task 5 Collating

The newsletter is to be completed by inserting the chart, information from the client's records and the fees for the use of the Club's facilities.

Database Assignment (solutions pages 101-102)

Clients' details

1 Using the Health and Fitness Club enrolment cards, create a database using appropriate fields and abbreviations, where necessary.

2 Store the data and print one copy in alphabetical order of surname.

3 Search the records and print the following:

a Surname, forename and category of membership, of all those who have stated that snooker is their main interest.

b Surname, full address and date of birth of all the females in the "Young Adult" category, who are specially interested in Gym.

c Full name, category and interest of all those members for whom you have no address.

HEALTH AND FITNESS CLUB

SURNAME KIRK FORENAME Brian

ADDRESS MALE/FEMALE

Road/Street 10 FISH ROW

Town SALISBURY

DoB 13.09.37

CATEGORY) A - Adult) YA - Young Adult) J - Junior

MAIN INTEREST Snooker

HEALTH AND FITNESS CLUB

SURNAME IRONSIDE FORENAME Paul

ADDRESS MALE/FEMALE

Road/Street 47 The Cutting

Town SALISBURY

DoB 15 07 76

CATEGORY) A - Adult) YA - Young Adult) J - Junior

MAIN INTEREST Gym

HEALTH AND FITNESS CLUB

SURNAME CHRISTIE FORENAME Christine

ADDRESS MALE/FEMALE

Road/Street 36 Duryard

Town DURRINGTON

DoB 16.12.70

CATEGORY) A - Adult) YA - Young Adult) J - Junior

MAIN INTEREST Sauna

HEALTH AND FITNESS CLUB

SURNAME MICHAELS FORENAME Janet

ADDRESS MALE/FEMALE

Road/Street 12 Red Bank

Town WILTON

DoB 3 March 1945

CATEGORY) A - Adult ✓) YA - Young Adult) J - Junior

MAIN INTEREST Sauna

HEALTH AND FITNESS CLUB

SURNAME OASCHE .... FORENAME Ben

ADDRESS .... MALE/FEMALE ✓

Road/Street Tree Tops

Town Durrington

DoB 15/6/46

(A) - Adult

CATEGORY) YA - Young Adult

) J - Junior

MAIN INTEREST Squash

HEALTH AND FITNESS CLUB

SURNAME SALISBURY .... FORENAME Michael

ADDRESS .... (MALE)/FEMALE

Road/Street 15 Fish Row

Town WILTON

DoB 10.10.64

) A - Adult

CATEGORY (YA) - Young Adult

) J - Junior

MAIN INTEREST SQUASH

HEALTH AND FITNESS CLUB

SURNAME BENTLEY .... FORENAME Maureen

ADDRESS .... MALE/(FEMALE)

Road/Street The Beeches

Town WILTON

DoB 25 December 1968

) A - Adult

CATEGORY (YA) - Young Adult

) J - Junior

MAIN INTEREST Squash

HEALTH AND FITNESS CLUB

SURNAME FRIEND .... FORENAME JO

ADDRESS .... MALE/(FEMALE)

Road/Street 19 High Rise

Town WILTON

DoB 11 June 1968

) A - Adult

CATEGORY (YA) - Young Adult

) J - Junior

MAIN INTEREST Sauna

HEALTH AND FITNESS CLUB

SURNAME CURTIS .... FORENAME DAVID

ADDRESS .... (MALE)/FEMALE

Road/Street 26 HIGH RISE

Town WILTON

DoB 15.10.60

(A) - Adult

CATEGORY) YA - Young Adult

) J - Junior

MAIN INTEREST SAUNA

HEALTH AND FITNESS CLUB

SURNAME Malineau .... FORENAME Barbara

ADDRESS .... MALE/(FEMALE)

Road/Street 263 Far Road

Town Wilton

DoB 12/3/63

) A - Adult

CATEGORY (YA) - Young Adult

) J - Junior

MAIN INTEREST Sauna

HEALTH AND FITNESS CLUB

SURNAME WORT FORENAME Chris

ADDRESS MALE/FEMALE

Road/Street 15 The Terrace

Town Salisbury

DoB 2.2.1950

(A) Adult

CATEGORY (YA) Young Adult

( ) J - Junior

MAIN INTEREST Squash

HEALTH AND FITNESS CLUB

SURNAME ENGLISH FORENAME Sue

ADDRESS MALE/FEMALE

Road/Street 21 Mary Hollow

Town Durrington

DoB 3 June 1978

( ) A - Adult

CATEGORY ( )YA - Young Adult

(J) Junior

MAIN INTEREST Gym

HEALTH AND FITNESS CLUB

SURNAME KING FORENAME Louise

ADDRESS MALE/FEMALE

Road/Street 15 Kite Street

Town SALISBURY

DoB 10 May 1973

( ) A - Adult

CATEGORY ( )YA - Young Adult

(J) Junior

MAIN INTEREST Gymnasium

HEALTH AND FITNESS CLUB

SURNAME FORMAN FORENAME DAVID

ADDRESS MALE/FEMALE

Road/Street 17 KITE STREET

Town SALISBURY

DoB 15 MARCH 1973

( ) A - Adult

CATEGORY ( )YA - Young Adult

(J) Junior

MAIN INTEREST GYM

HEALTH AND FITNESS CLUB

SURNAME THOMAS FORENAME Thomas

ADDRESS MALE/FEMALE

Road/Street 15 DURYARD

Town DURRINGTON

DoB 19 JUNE 1965

( ) A - Adult

CATEGORY (YA) Young Adult

( ) J - Junior

MAIN INTEREST SAUNA

HEALTH AND FITNESS CLUB

SURNAME JONES FORENAME CHRISTOPHER (CHRIS)

ADDRESS MALE/FEMALE

Road/Street 15 HILL GARDENS

Town WILTON

DoB 23 JULY 1959

(A) Adult

CATEGORY ( )YA - Young Adult

( ) J - Junior

MAIN INTEREST SQUASH

HEALTH AND FITNESS CLUB

SURNAME SMITH FORENAME Walter

ADDRESS .... MALE/FEMALE (MALE circled)

Road/Street ?

Town ....

DoB August 12th 1950

(A) - Adult (circled)

CATEGORY) YA - Young Adult

) J - Junior

MAIN INTEREST Snooker

HEALTH AND FITNESS CLUB

SURNAME Briant FORENAME Rachel

ADDRESS .... MALE/FEMALE (FEMALE circled)

Road/Street 7 Sussex Square

Town DURRINGTON

DoB 3 January 1971

) A - Adult

CATEGORY (YA) - Young Adult (circled)

) J - Junior

MAIN INTEREST Gym

HEALTH AND FITNESS CLUB

SURNAME BEST FORENAME Amanda

ADDRESS .... MALE/FEMALE (FEMALE circled)

Road/Street 26 The Mill

Town DURRINGTON

DoB 6.12.43

)(A) Adult (circled)

CATEGORY) YA - Young Adult

) J - Junior

MAIN INTEREST Sauna

HEALTH AND FITNESS CLUB

SURNAME THOMPSON FORENAME Brinda

ADDRESS .... MALE/FEMALE ✓

Road/Street 26 Duwon Road

Town WILTON

DoB 30.12.60

)(A) Adult (circled)

CATEGORY) YA - Young Adult

) J - Junior

MAIN INTEREST Snooker

HEALTH AND FITNESS CLUB

SURNAME THOMPSON FORENAME Phillip

ADDRESS .... MALE/FEMALE (MALE circled)

Road/Street 26 Duwon Road

Town WILTON

DoB 30.11.59

)(A) Adult (circled)

CATEGORY) YA - Young Adult

) J - Junior

MAIN INTEREST Squash

HEALTH AND FITNESS CLUB

SURNAME GREGORY FORENAME Fredrick

ADDRESS .... MALE/FEMALE (FEMALE crossed out)

Road/Street 126 Fish Row

Town SALISBURY

DoB 24.07.38

) A - Adult

CATEGORY Adult) YA - Young Adult

) J - Junior

MAIN INTEREST Snooker

HEALTH AND FITNESS CLUB

SURNAME HESSAYON FORENAME George

ADDRESS MALE/~~FEMALE~~

Road/Street 15 ~~Evercoming Cres~~ Brown Close

Town SALISBURY

DoB 13.06.40

CATEGORY A

) A - Adult
)YA - Young Adult
) J - Junior

MAIN INTEREST Gymnasium

HEALTH AND FITNESS CLUB

SURNAME MANNING FORENAME [illegible]

ADDRESS MALE/FEMALE

Road/Street 26 Barnaby Road

Town SALISBURY

DoB 13.12.50

CATEGORY

(A) - Adult (circled)
)YA - Young Adult
) J - Junior

MAIN INTEREST Squash

HEALTH AND FITNESS CLUB

SURNAME Manning FORENAME Alan

ADDRESS (MALE)/FEMALE

Road/Street 26 Barnaby Rd

Town Salisbury

DoB 02.06.48

CATEGORY

(A) Adult (circled)
)YA - Young Adult
) J - Junior

MAIN INTEREST Squash

HEALTH AND FITNESS CLUB

SURNAME HOLLAND FORENAME Pauline

ADDRESS MALE/FE(MALE)

Road/Street ~~11 St Marys Hollow~~ 11 Mary Hollow

Town DURRINGTON

DoB 15 February 1970

CATEGORY

) A - Adult
(YA) - Young Adult (circled)
) J - Junior

MAIN INTEREST Gym

HEALTH AND FITNESS CLUB

SURNAME POINTER FORENAME Elizabeth

ADDRESS MALE/(FEMALE)

Road/Street 90 Sunset Drive

Town DURRINGTON

DoB 26 June 1971

CATEGORY

) A - Adult
(YA) - Young Adult (circled)
) J - Junior

MAIN INTEREST gym

HEALTH AND FITNESS CLUB

SURNAME SMITH FORENAME Anne

ADDRESS MALE/FEMALE (ticked)

Road/Street ?

Town

DoB ?

CATEGORY

) A - Adult
(YA) - Young Adult (circled)
) J - Junior

MAIN INTEREST Snooker

HEALTH AND FITNESS CLUB

SURNAME SMITH FORENAME Harold

ADDRESS .... MALE/FEMALE

Road/Street ?

Town ....

DoB ?

) A - Adult

CATEGORY)YA - Young Adult

) J - Junior

MAIN INTEREST Snooker.

HEALTH AND FITNESS CLUB

SURNAME DAVIS FORENAME Simon

ADDRESS .... MALE/FEMALE

Road/Street 22 Gas Lane

Town WILTON

DoB 15 Sep 1977

) A - Adult

CATEGORY)YA - Young Adult

) J - Junior

MAIN INTEREST Gym

HEALTH AND FITNESS CLUB

SURNAME CARDING FORENAME Matthew

ADDRESS .... MALE/FEMALE

Road/Street 106 Far Road

Town WILTON

DoB 10 June 1976

) A - Adult

CATEGORY)YA - Young Adult

) J - Junior

MAIN INTEREST Gym

HEALTH AND FITNESS CLUB

SURNAME WELDON FORENAME Francis

ADDRESS .... MALE/FEMALE

Road/Street 10 The Mill

Town DURRINGTON

DoB 3 August 1976

) A - Adult

CATEGORY)YA - Young Adult

) J - Junior

MAIN INTEREST Gym

HEALTH AND FITNESS CLUB

SURNAME SIMMONDS FORENAME Anne

ADDRESS .... MALE/FEMALE ✓

Road/Street 10 The Mill

Town DURRINGTON

DoB 3.10.70

) A - Adult

CATEGORY)YA - Young Adult

) J - Junior

MAIN INTEREST Squash

Spreadsheet Assignment (solutions pages 103-108)

Financial information

The following financial statistics are all that are available for the first year of operation of the Health and Fitness Club. Unfortunately, although records were kept, a fire destroyed all paperwork at the end of the year, and the management would like to reconstruct some figures as a basis on which to work for the future.

You are advised to divide the figures under two headings - Income and Expenditure - and incorporate all the information given.

1 Enter the data.

2 Save the data and print a copy of the whole spreadsheet showing profit or loss as appropriate.

3 The management feels that only a small profit was made, and steps need to be taken to improve this in the second year:

a Print out the section of the spreadsheet which would show the fees per session, and the weekly receipts. Make sure you include the names of the facilities.

b What would be the position if the Club managed to attract 10 per cent more clients in all categories? Make the necessary amendments, and print out a copy of the whole spreadsheet.

c Assuming the extra clients do join, what effect would be produced by increasing fees by 20p for the use of all facilities? Print a copy of the resulting spreadsheet.

d The management are hoping to incorporate a swimming pool in the rebuilding project. Assume membership as in (c) above. The proposed fee will be £2.00 per session (all age groups). Assume all members attend for at least one session each week.

Make the necessary adjustments to the spreadsheet, and print a copy.

4 Print another copy of the final spreadsheet showing the formulae.

Financial Statistics

Annual subscription

Adult	£115
Young Adult	£70
Junior	£30

Fees for use of facilities

Squash (per adult per session)	£2.05
Squash (per young adult per session)	£1.75
Squash (per junior per session)	£1.10
Gymnasium (per adult per session)	£2.05
Gymnasium (per young adult per session)	£1.75
Gymnasium (per junior per session)	£1.10
Snooker (per table per session)	£3.50
Sauna (per person per session)	£2.05

Other income

Average bar takings each night	£250
Average restaurant takings each night	£250

The club is open seven days a week, and 52 weeks a year.

There are currently 350 adult members, 120 young adults and 50 junior members.

Seventy-five per cent of members attend the club at least once a week to use the squash courts or gymnasium.

The snooker table is booked every day throughout the week, the normal usage being five sessions per day.

The sauna is increasingly popular and on average is used for 15 sessions per day, usually by five members at a time.

Twenty-five specialist staff are employed at a salary of £200 per week each. Five cleaners are employed and they earn £50 each per week.

Electricity and other outgoings amount to £1000 weekly.

Note: When calculating income other than subscriptions, you will find it more convenient to work first to a weekly figure and then to an annual figure, ie weekly figure multiplied by 52 (weeks in a year).

Word Processing Assignment (solution pages 109-110)

Members' newsletter

1 Create a file using single line spacing and justified right-hand margin.

2 Enter the following text and number the pages.

3 Save and print.

Health & Fitness Club ← Centre & embolden heading
Newsletter ← centre & underline

(1st Para in DLS please)

The Health & Fitness Club offers a superior gymnasium and excellent facilities for indoor leisure activities. Since the recent fire, the Club has ~~recently~~ been substantially improved to meet the recreational needs of the next decade.

Squash, snooker & pool are among the sports played at the Club. In addition there is a superb ~~gym~~ training gymnasium with fitness circuitry equipment and exercise cycles, plus a sauna.

The Club is situated in an ideal ~~spot~~ location, close to main roads, with plentiful car parking. It is housed in an ~~attractive~~ architecturally pleasing building by one of the city's picturesque rivers. ~~Car parking is~~

The Club is open (seven days a week,) from 9.00am to 11.00pm, ⋏

Charges

Charges for facilities are detailed below:

↓ leave 6 line spaces here

~~Insert Errolling here~~

Facilities

Squash Courts | Gymnasium | Sauna
Snooker Room | Sports Shop | Licensed Bar
Lounge | Coaching | Riverside Restaurant

Five Squash Courts

All courts are ~~built of~~ constructed to the highest standards including ~~fully~~ sprung spring beechwood floors. Tuition & coaching is ~~given~~ provided by two approved professional coaches.

Gymnasium

The ~~&~~ Gymnasium incorporates the ~~very~~ latest exercise & fitness equipment in a well laid out environment with a view overlooking the river.

~~Staff qualified in physical education are on hand to instruct & supervise in the use of equipment, and aerobics classes also form part of the regular~~ fitness schedules.

Sauna

A splendid ~~new~~ 12-person Nordic (NORDIC) sauna is available for the ultimate in health-promoting relaxation, together with its own shower ~~in immediate proximity~~ immediately adjacent. ~~to it~~.

Snooker Room

A full-size championship snooker ~~table~~ and billiards table provides members with a relaxing alternative to more strenuous exercise. // Our ~~Shop~~ Sports Shop stocks a generous range of sports equipment, and advice on rackets and specialist equipment is / always available. N.P.

embolden Sports Shop

embolden L. Bar please

The Licensed Bar is large & centrally positioned. It is open throughout the day with coffee & soft drinks always available. A ~~different~~ varied menu is on offer in our newly completed Restaurant area, much of the food being homemade.

(Embolden Restaurant & Lounge)

The Lounge adjoins the bar and provides ~~cosy~~ comfortable seating with views over the garden & river. There is a small television area and daily papers and current sporting periodicals are ~~there~~ available for members' use.

<u>Enrolling</u>

A sample of our enrolment record card is given below, & you will see that we have dispensed with long, complicated enrolment forms, which ask you so many intimate & often seemingly unnecessary details. We are sure you will agree this is a great advantage.

~~leave 6 lines for later insertion~~

STOP PRESS (Caps & margin)

Since the fire we have managed to reorganise most of our paperwork, but the Management would be grateful if the following people could contact them as soon as possible.

Graphics Assignment (solution page 111)

Members' categories

1 Using the Financial Statistics create and label a chart showing the numbers of each category of members currently enrolled in the Club.

2 The chart should be entitled Current Membership.

3 Label the x-axis Adult, Young Adult and Junior, or use suitable abbreviations.

4 Save and print the display.

Collating Assignment (solution page 112-114)

Members' newsletter

1 Recall the word processing file you created earlier.

2 After the line about the Club opening times, insert the graphical representation or attach a copy of the diagram to the end of the document, as Appendix A, with *an appropriate note in the text.*

* 3 After the paragraph headed Charges insert the section of the spreadsheet showing fees for the use of facilities.

* 4 At the end of the document, after Stop Press insert the list from the database which shows those members for whom no address is currently available.

5 If necessary, repaginate and renumber the pages.

6 Present the final document.

Note * These items must *not be re-keyed*, but should be included by:

a using integrated software to collate the different sections;

b printing out the extracts separately from the word processed document and then sticking them in at the appropriate places; OR

c using desktop publishing facilities.

3 Publishing Company

Scenario

The Citizen Publishing Company has grown from a small company started over one hundred years ago, to a major producer of quality books. It is dedicated to producing work of a high standard and publishes mainly novels, travel and educational books. You have been asked to assist with the following tasks:

Task 1 Database

Create a file of all books published over the last few years in order that the management may search the data to find specific groups of titles.

Task 2 Spreadsheet

Produce a spreadsheet giving all the financial information about books published in 1994.

Task 3 Word Processing

Start to compile the yearly newsletter giving a short history of the company, information about authors' royalties and news on current sales.

Task 4 Graphics

Produce a graph illustrating comparative figures for Home and Export Sales for a given year.

Task 5 Collating

Complete the newsletter by inserting information taken from the graphics file and the relevant data from the database and spreadsheet.

Database Assignment (solutions page 115)

Publications

1 Using the information contained in the Source Documents create a database with each record containing the following fields:

Ref No
Title
Author (surname only required)
First published
Category
Cost per copy

Use the following two-letter code in the Category field:

Educational - ED
Novel - NO
Travel - TR

2 Save the information.

3 Print the whole file in column form.

4 Sort the file into alphabetical order for title, and print the whole file.

5 Search the file for all the educational books first published in 1994, and print the Ref No, Title and Author name only.

6 Find all the Travel books by Hendrik, published in 1994 and print the Ref No, Title and Author only.

SOURCE DOCUMENTS

Book cost:

Reference Initial	Cost per copy
E	£10.99
T	£12.50
N	£15.00

Author's royalties:

10% for all books

RECENT PUBLICATIONS

CATALOGUE REF NO	TITLE	AUTHOR	PUBLISHED
T-234760	Too Many Cooks	Bake, U	1993
E-339211	How To Get On at Maths	Entwhistle, B	1993
T-234339	Three Miles Down	Deeping, W	1994
N-100662	I Love Life	Mann, J	1993
N-100633	Wassername!	Tremelowe, L	1993
E-339134	So you bought a computer?	Hacker, A	1994
E-339857	Maths, Glorious Maths	Entwhistle, B	1994
N-100997	Come in Number Three	Spooner, C	1993
N-100108	The Last Laugh	Mann, J	1992
E-339687	Using your computer	Hacker, A	1993
T-234397	Up the Creek!	Hendrik, B	1994
T-234551	Living with Crocodiles	Deeping, W	1992
E-339996	English for Eggheads	Cawson, R	1993
N-100304	The Way to the Moon	Pernelle, K	1994
E-339400	Easy ways to study	Roughman, W	1993
N-100366	Dead Ringer!	Stowell, S	1994
N-100367	Pigeon Pie	Sansome, S	1994
T-234900	Down among the Deadmen	Hendrik, B	1992
T-234588	Living with Rhinos	Deeping, W	1993
T-234600	Elephant infants	Deeping, W	1993
E-339807	Logarithms made easy	Entwhistle, B	1992
E-339898	French fantasia	Martine, M	1994
N-100122	The Master Calls	Sansome, P	1993
N-100555	Fancy That!	Stowell, S	1993
T-234650	Timbuctoo Overland	Hendrik, B	1994
T-234700	Zulu Country	Deeping, W	1992
E-339760	Gentle German	Witz, W	1994
E-339667	Teach yourself Japanese	Ying, Y	1993
E-339520	Multiplication madness	Entwhistle, B	1994

CATALOGUE REF NO	HOME SALES	EXPORT SALES
EDUCATIONAL		
E-339211	3000	250
E-339134	1980	69
E-339857	2543	150
E-339867	3100	192
E-339996	1995	89
E-339400	1320	230
E-339807	900	90
E-339898	500	20
E-339760	675	56
E-339667	1000	250
E-339520	1864	98
NOVELS		
N-100662	5600	500
N-100633	4504	237
N-100997	6003	1000
N-100108	2580	243
N-100304	7343	312
N-100366	5650	1055
N-100367	4340	1200
N-100122	5000	1250
N-100555	3420	250
TRAVEL		
T-234760	1000	100
T-234339	1565	65
T-234397	2330	245
T-234551	3005	300
T-234900	1246	245
T-234588	1080	89
T-234600	2004	58
T-234650	1986	406
T-234700	980	35

Spreadsheet Assignment (solutions page 116)

Sales information

1 Using the information contained in the Source Documents construct a spreadsheet. Include only the figures for those books first published in 1994.

Insert a main title: 1994 Publications

2 Include the following information:

Ref No (initial and last 3 digits only required, eg T760)
Author surname
No. of Home Sales
No. of Export Sales
Combined Sales

3 Enter the information, and, using a formula, calculate the total for both the Home and Export Sales.

4 Calculate the numbers of each book sold both at home and overseas, and provide an overall total.

5 Print the data.

6 Calculate the amount of royalties due to each author for each book and provide a final figure for the total amount of royalties paid out in 1994.

7 Print two copies of the spreadsheet - one showing the figures and the other showing the formulae used.

8 Next year royalties may be raised to 12%. Make this amendment, and print only the totals for Home and Export Sales, Combined Sales and the final Royalty Figure.

Word Processing Assignment (solution pages 117-118)

Newsletter

1 Create a file using single line spacing and a line length of 65 characters.

2 Enter the following text with an unjustified right margin, and number the pages.

3 Save and print.

← at margin

← THE CITIZEN PUBLISHING COMPANY

← Yearly Newsletter (underline please)

First Paragraph & 2nd in DLS & bold please

As you know we are committed to publishing quality books covering a ~~wide~~ variety of subjects and ~~we~~ are proud to send you our latest fully illustrated, colour ~~price list~~ catalogue which we hope you will peruse with interest.

Our publishing house was ~~star~~ founded in 1890 and we have now celebrated over 100 years of service to the discerning reader. Our founder opened his first business in a small shed at the back of his own house using a hand-operated printing press. However, trade was so good, ~~because~~ owing to the quality of his work, that he quickly outgrew those meagre premises, and the present purpose-built premises were erected on this site.

EXECUTIVE STAFF

General Manager	James MacKenzie	Ext 100
Chief Desk Editor	Alan Triscombe	Ext 201
Typesetter	Joe Mancewicz	Ext 350
Secretary	Helen Bryant	Ext 101

AUTHORS' ROYALTIES

At the beginning of this year we were worried that, owing to the general financial situation in the country as a whole, we may have had to reduce prices ~~royalties~~.

However, we are happy to say that we have been able to maintain the percentage paid to ~~all~~ authors, and are even hoping to increase the amount paid, perhaps by 2%. Our Accountant is even now investigating the possibility, and the following figures illustrate the effect:

(leave 1" here please)

PUBLICATIONS

The majority of our ~~books~~ publications can be classified into 3 main categories: Education, Travel and Novels, and the figure below illustrates graphically which sections of our publishing have been more successful than others. You will ~~notice~~ see that Novels are extremely successful in the Home Sales market, while Education & Travel are 'struggling'.

(leave ~~1½"~~ 1" here)

What is immediately apparent from this graph and is a very worrying aspect, is the very low incidence of export sales in all categories. The Management has already ~~is~~ launched a special investigation into the problem and the Committee ~~are~~ is due to report in a few weeks.

AND NOW THE GOOD NEWS!

All is not doom & gloom, however, & although sales figures are not all we had hoped for the number of educational books published during the year is very encouraging.

leave 1" here

You will see that Brian Entwhistle continues to write for us, & his books are always popular in schools - especially with the introduction of 'GNVQ - A Mathematical Approach', and 'Maths is Fun', both books being scheduled for publication early next year.

We also have a number of new writers currently preparing text for other areas of GNVQ and shall be issuing further details in the near future.

Graphics Assignment (solution page 119)

Comparative sales

1 Using figures from the spreadsheet which you created earlier, construct a graph showing comparative figures for Home and Export Sales.

2 Use a main heading: Books Published

3 Use a sub-heading: 1994

4 Use suitable titles on the x axis and y axis, and add a legend if necessary to illustrate the graph.

Collating Assignment (solution pages 120-122)

Newsletter

1 Using the document produced in the word processing assignment, add the following to the text:

* a From the spreadsheet

After the paragraphs referring to Authors' Royalties insert the totals as a result of the proposed increase to 12%.

* b From the graphics

Insert your graphical representation after the first paragraph of "Publications" - or attach a copy of the diagram to the end of the document, as Appendix A with *an appropriate note in the text.*

* c From the database

After the first paragraph of the Good News section of the document, insert the Ref No, Title and Author of books published during the year.

2 If necessary repaginate and renumber the pages.

3 Present the final document.

Note: * These items must *not be re-keyed*, but should be included by:

a using integrated software to collate the different sections;

b printing out the extracts separately from the word processed document and then sticking them in at the appropriate places; OR

c using desktop publishing facilities.

4 *Horticultural Show*

Scenario

The Horticultural Show was formed several years ago, and has taken place in the county regularly ever since. This year the Committee has planned a number of innovations.

In addition to the marquee with its now-famous exhibits, a variety of entertainment has been arranged to take place throughout the day. You have been asked to help with the organisation by carrying out the following tasks.

Task 1 Database

You need to begin by setting up a database containing records of plants. The information will be made available to members and will also be used as a basis for a competition.

Task 2 Spreadsheet

The costs of mounting such a large exhibition are rising yearly. The Chairperson wants details of expenditure for the last few years, together with some idea of how costs might rise in the future.

Task 3 Word Processing

All local associations are sent details of the forthcoming show, to create interest amongst their members. Please type a copy of the rough notes prepared by the Secretary.

Task 4 Graphics

Produce a pie chart showing entries for the last five years for one specific section of the schedule.

Task 5 Collating

Complete the circular to local associations by inserting the graphics, the list of flowers for the competition, and details of the entry fees for the last few years.

Database Assignment (solutions pages 123-124)

Plant profiles

1 Refer to the Plant Profile cards and create a database file. Each record should include the following:

Name of plant

Colour

Type of plant: Perennial
Half-hardy annual
Wild
Hardy annual

Plant height (enter all heights in cm)

Position: Warm sheltered
Shady
Sunny
Most

2 Save the data.

3 Search the information and print the following lists:

a The whole file in alphabetical order of plant name.

b All the information for any yellow flowering perennial plants which will grow in most positions.

c Height and name of any plant which is 20 cm and under.

d All the information on the yellow flowering plants.

e The names and suitable position of all the flowers which are available in mixed colours.

f The names, colours and height of all the plants which will grow in a shady corner of the garden.

g Names and colours of half-hardy annuals which will grow in a warm, sheltered place.

PLANT PROFILES

PLANT NAME Dog Rose

COLOUR Pink

HEIGHT 3 metres

POSITION WS – Warm sheltered) please circle
SH – Shady) appropriate
S – Sunny) abbreviation
M – Most)

TYPE P – Perennial
HHA – Half Hardy Annual
WD – Wild
HA – Hardy Annual

Price 75 p

PLANT PROFILES

PLANT NAME STOCK

COLOUR PINK

HEIGHT 70

POSITION WS – Warm sheltered) please circle
SH – Shady) appropriate
S – Sunny) abbreviation
M – Most)

TYPE P – Perennial
HHA – Half Hardy Annual ✓
WD – Wild
HA – Hardy Annual

Price ....

PLANT PROFILES

PLANT NAME Mimulus

COLOUR Orange

HEIGHT 28

POSITION WS – Warm sheltered) please circle
SH – Shady) appropriate
S – Sunny) abbreviation
M – Most)

TYPE P – Perennial
HHA – Half Hardy Annual
WD – Wild
HA – Hardy Annual

Price ....

PLANT PROFILES

PLANT NAME Petunia

COLOUR Red

HEIGHT 30

POSITION WS – Warm sheltered) please circle
SH – Shady) appropriate
S – Sunny) abbreviation
M – Most ✓)

TYPE P – Perennial
HHA – Half Hardy Annual
WD – Wild
HA – Hardy Annual

Price ....

PLANT PROFILES

PLANT NAME PANSY

COLOUR MIXED

HEIGHT 15

POSITION WS – Warm sheltered) please circle
SH – Shady) appropriate
S – Sunny) abbreviation
M – Most Any)

TYPE P – Perennial
HHA – Half Hardy Annual
WD – Wild
HA – Hardy Annual

Price 65p

PLANT PROFILES

PLANT NAME Dimorphotheca

COLOUR Yellow

HEIGHT 30cm

POSITION WS – Warm sheltered) please circle
SH – Shady) appropriate
S – Sunny) abbreviation
M – Most)

TYPE P – Perennial
HHA – Half Hardy Annual
WD – Wild
HA – Hardy Annual

Price 65p

PLANT PROFILES

PLANT NAME TROLLIUS

COLOUR YELLOW

HEIGHT 40 cm

POSITION WS – Warm sheltered) please circle
SH – Shady) appropriate
S – Sunny) abbreviation
M – Most)

TYPE P – Perennial
HHA – Half Hardy Annual
WD – Wild
HA – Hardy Annual
PERENNIAL

Price 57p

PLANT PROFILES

PLANT NAME Astilbe

COLOUR Cream

HEIGHT 200

POSITION WS – Warm sheltered) please circle
SH – Shady) appropriate
S – Sunny) abbreviation
M – Most)

TYPE P – Perennial
HHA – Half Hardy Annual
WD – Wild
HA – Hardy Annual

Price ....

PLANT PROFILES

PLANT NAME ECHINOPS

COLOUR BLUE

HEIGHT 100

POSITION WS – Warm sheltered) please circle
SH – Shady) appropriate
S – Sunny) abbreviation
M – Most)

TYPE P – Perennial
HHA – Half Hardy Annual
WD – Wild
HA – Hardy Annual

Price ....

PLANT PROFILES

PLANT NAME VERBENA

COLOUR ~~SCARLET~~ RED

HEIGHT 30

POSITION WS – Warm sheltered) please circle
SH – Shady) appropriate
S – Sunny) abbreviation
M – Most)

TYPE P – Perennial
HHA – Half Hardy Annual
WD – Wild
HA – Hardy Annual

Price ....

PLANT PROFILES

PLANT NAME Primrose

COLOUR Yellow

HEIGHT 15 cm

POSITION WS – Warm sheltered) please circle
SH – Shady) appropriate
S – Sunny ✓) abbreviation
M – Most)

TYPE P – Perennial
HHA – Half Hardy Annual
WD – Wild ✓
HA – Hardy Annual

Price £0.95

PLANT PROFILES

PLANT NAME Catmint

COLOUR Blue

HEIGHT 40 cm

POSITION WS – Warm sheltered) please circle
SH – Shady) appropriate
S – Sunny) abbreviation
M – Most)

TYPE P – Perennial
HHA – Half Hardy Annual
WD – Wild
HA – Hardy Annual

Price 57p

PLANT PROFILES

PLANT NAME Dianthus

COLOUR White

HEIGHT 20 cm

POSITION (WS) – Warm sheltered) please circle
~~SH~~ – Shady) appropriate
S – Sunny) abbreviation
M – Most)

TYPE ~~P – Perennial~~
HHA – Half Hardy Annual ✓
~~WD – Wild~~
~~HA – Hardy Annual~~

Price £1.40

PLANT PROFILES

PLANT NAME COSMOS

COLOUR PINK

HEIGHT 1m

POSITION WS – Warm sheltered) please circle
SH – Shady) appropriate
S – Sunny ✓) abbreviation
M – Most)

TYPE P – Perennial
HHA – Half Hardy Annual ✓
WD – Wild
HA – Hardy Annual

Price ....

PLANT PROFILES

PLANT NAME Delphinium

COLOUR Blue

HEIGHT 130 cm

POSITION WS – Warm sheltered) please circle
SH – Shady) appropriate
S – Sunny ✓) abbreviation
M – Most)

TYPE P – Perennial
HHA – Half Hardy Annual
WD – Wild
HA – Hardy Annual ✓

Price ....

PLANT PROFILES

PLANT NAME GYPSOPHILA

COLOUR White

HEIGHT 36

POSITION WS – Warm sheltered) please circle
SH – Shady) appropriate
S – Sunny ✓) abbreviation
M – Most)

TYPE P – Perennial
HHA – Half Hardy Annual
WD – Wild
HA – Hardy Annual ✓

Price ....

PLANT PROFILES

PLANT NAME ANTIRRHINUM

COLOUR MIXED

HEIGHT 45 cm

POSITION (WS) – Warm sheltered) please circle
~~SH~~ – Shady) appropriate
S – Sunny) abbreviation
M – Most)

TYPE P – Perennial
(HHA) – Half Hardy Annual
~~WD~~ – Wild
HA – Hardy Annual

Price 65p

PLANT PROFILES

PLANT NAME Campanula

COLOUR Blue

HEIGHT 20 cm

POSITION (WS) – Warm sheltered) please circle
~~SH~~ – Shady) appropriate
S – Sunny) abbreviation
M – Most)

TYPE ~~P~~ – Perennial
(HHA) – Half Hardy Annual
~~WD~~ – Wild
HA – Hardy Annual

Price 2.15

PLANT PROFILES

PLANT NAME Foxglove

COLOUR Pink

HEIGHT 1m

POSITION WS – Warm sheltered) please circle
SH – Shady) appropriate
S – Sunny) abbreviation
M – Most)

TYPE P – Perennial
HHA – Half Hardy Annual
WD – Wild
HA – Hardy Annual

Price 55p

PLANT PROFILES

PLANT NAME HELICHRYSUM

COLOUR MIXED

HEIGHT 45 cm

POSITION ~~WS – Warm sheltered~~) please circle
~~SH – Shady~~) appropriate
S – Sunny) abbreviation
~~M – Most~~)

TYPE P – Perennial
HHA – Half Hardy Annual
WD – Wild
HA – Hardy Annual ✓

Price 50p

PLANT PROFILES

PLANT NAME SOLIDAGO

COLOUR YELLOW

HEIGHT 60cm

POSITION ~~WS – Warm sheltered~~) ~~please circle~~
~~SH – Shady~~) ~~appropriate~~
~~S – Sunny~~) ~~abbreviation~~
M – Most ✓)

Sorry!

TYPE P – Perennial
HHA – Half Hardy Annual
WD – Wild
HA – Hardy Annual

Price 53p

PLANT PROFILES

PLANT NAME Lupin

COLOUR mixed

HEIGHT 30cm

POSITION WS – Warm sheltered) please circle
SH – Shady) appropriate
S – Sunny) abbreviation
M – Most)

TYPE P – Perennial
HHA – Half Hardy Annual
WD – Wild
HA – Hardy Annual

Price 52p

PLANT PROFILES

PLANT NAME MECONOPSIS

COLOUR ~~RED~~ BLUE

HEIGHT 90 cm

POSITION WS – Warm sheltered) please circle
SH – Shady) appropriate
S – Sunny) abbreviation
M – Most)

TYPE P – Perennial
HHA – Half Hardy Annual
WD – Wild
HA – Hardy Annual

Price 1·45p

PLANT PROFILES

PLANT NAME Toadflax

COLOUR yellow

HEIGHT 60 cm high

POSITION WS – Warm sheltered) please circle
SH – Shady) appropriate
S – Sunny) abbreviation
M – Most)

TYPE P – Perennial
HHA – Half Hardy Annual
WD – Wild
HA – Hardy Annual

Price 65p

PLANT PROFILES

PLANT NAME CYCLAMEN

COLOUR PINK

HEIGHT 15

POSITION WS – Warm sheltered) please circle
SH – Shady) appropriate
S – Sunny) abbreviation
M – Most)

TYPE P – Perennial
HHA – Half Hardy Annual
WD – Wild
HA – Hardy Annual

Price 1·30p

PLANT PROFILES

PLANT NAME Hosta

COLOUR green

HEIGHT 60 cm

POSITION WS – Warm sheltered) please circle
SH – Shady) appropriate
S – Sunny) abbreviation
M – Most)

TYPE P – Perennial
HHA – Half Hardy Annual
WD – Wild
HA – Hardy Annual

Price 1·15p

PLANT PROFILES

PLANT NAME Cineraria

COLOUR Silver

HEIGHT 20 cm

POSITION WS – Warm sheltered) please circle
SH – Shady) appropriate
S – Sunny) abbreviation
M – Most)

TYPE P – Perennial
HHA – Half Hardy Annual
WD – Wild
HA – Hardy Annual

Price 65p

PLANT PROFILES

PLANT NAME ALSTROMERIA

COLOUR PINK

HEIGHT 75 cm

POSITION WS – Warm sheltered) please circle
SH – Shady) appropriate
S – Sunny) abbreviation
M – Most)

TYPE P – Perennial ✓
HHA – Half Hardy Annual
WD – Wild
HA – Hardy Annual

Price 1·05

PLANT PROFILES

PLANT NAME Semperflorens

COLOUR ~~15cm~~ mixed

HEIGHT 15 cm

POSITION WS – Warm sheltered) please circle
SH – Shady) appropriate
S – Sunny) abbreviation
M – Most)

TYPE P – Perennial
HHA – Half Hardy Annual
WD – Wild
HA – Hardy Annual

Price £ 1·47

PLANT PROFILES

PLANT NAME ACHILLEA

COLOUR YELLOW

HEIGHT 150cm

POSITION WS – Warm sheltered) please circle
SH – Shady) appropriate
S – Sunny) abbreviation
M – Most)

TYPE P – Perennial
HHA – Half Hardy Annual
WD – Wild
HA – Hardy Annual

Price 65p

PLANT PROFILES

PLANT NAME Sunflower

COLOUR Yellow

HEIGHT 2m!

POSITION WS – Warm sheltered) please circle
SH – Shady) appropriate
S – Sunny) abbreviation
M – Most)

TYPE P – Perennial
HHA – Half Hardy Annual
WD – Wild
HA – Hardy Annual

Price 46p

Spreadsheet Assignment (solutions pages 125-127)

County Horticultural Show costs

1 Using the details on the financial statistics sheet, create a spreadsheet using the title: County Horticultural Show. Display the figures in two sections (Income and Expenditure). The Income section must include Entry Fees, Number of Entrants in each class, Income from Sales and Total Income.

The Expenditure section must include all the costs given and additionally an annual figure for Profit/Loss.

Use the years for the column headings. REMEMBER - this is the fifth year of the Show.

2 Enter the data.

3 Save and print the spreadsheet.

4 Print another copy of the spreadsheet showing the formulae.

5 The Committee wishes to know what the financial position would be next year if the following figures applied:

a Entry fees remain the same as this year.

b No. of entrants remains the same as this year.

c Sales rise by 5%.

d Printing and engraving remain at £150.

e Hire of marquee is increased to £356.

f Judges' fees remain the same as this year.

Insert another column headed for next year and recalculate the totals.

6 Print a copy of the whole projected spreadsheet for comparison purposes.

Financial Statistics

Income

Entry fees:

In the Show's first year, Entry Fees were 50p for vegetable classes, 40p for flower classes and 30p for handicraft classes. Fees rose in all classes by 10p in each of the following two years, and by 20p in each of the next two years.

No. of Entrants	1st Year	2nd Year	3rd Year	4th Year	This Year
Vegetables	120	125	156	160	160
Flowers	200	220	255	280	300
Handicrafts	90	100	120	125	150

Sales

Sales from all sources raised £200 in the first year and have risen by 5% each year.

Expenditure

Printing and engraving - £150 per year.

Hire of marquee - £250 each year.

Judges' fees - costs were £80 the first year and rose by 2.5% in each subsequent year.

Word Processing Assignment (solution pages 128-129)

Chairperson's circular

1 Create a file using single line spacing and justified right-hand margin.

2 Enter the following text and number the pages.

3 Save and print.

COUNTY HORTICULTURAL SHOW

Please include Committee Members here

(Centre & embolden heading)

DOUBLE LINE SPACING HERE

We are proud to present our schedule for the forthcoming horticultural show, & we think you will agree that it is the most exciting in the history of the Show. We have ~~kept~~ retained all the old familiar classes which have proved to be popular with you all over the past years; but we have included several new (and perhaps a little unusual) classes, which have been suggested to us by entrants - these are numbered 104-109 in the schedule and we hope you will find them interesting and challenging. Please let the Committee know your thoughts on these innovations and also let us know if you have any constructive suggestions or new ideas.

ENTRIES ← leave a line space here

Entries in all classes have been rising steadily since ~~1984~~ our first year and we are particularly pleased with the increase in the Handicraft entries, as these started off so hesit~~a~~tantly in the first year.

(leave 12 lines here)

ENTRY FEES ← leave a line here.

The committee have decided that because the entry fees have risen steadily over the last few years, it is advisable to ~~reinstate~~ retain the present ~~the present~~ level, and not increase them again. A recommendation is to be put to the next AGM to the effect that fees should be "frozen" at the present level, at least for the next two years.

(leave 6 lines here for insertion of SS details)

ENTERTAINMENT ← leave a line

The organisation for this year's show is progressing satisfactorily, & the Secretary has already booked several people ~~to~~ who are coming to display their crafts. Amongst these is the local potter, Michelle Destang, whose work ~~is currently being exhibited~~ has been chosen for display by a very famous London store; and Terry Michell with his beautiful long case clocks, all ~~lovi~~ lovingly made by hand.

We also hope to have a dancing display by the "Irish Shamrocks", the newly formed dancing ~~troupe~~ troupe, as well as a demonstration of dog handling by the Police Dog Association and pony rides for the children. Altogether, we ~~hope~~ are sure you will agree, a good mixture for a successful day.

Please include COMPETITION here.

LAYOUT OF ~~SIGHT~~ SITE

(✓) We are ~~very~~ quite fortunate this year in having obtained the services of Lt Col Brian Chichester, who is organising the layout of the site. Those of you who attended the show last year will remember that ~~one or two~~ one or two of the outside exhibitors' stands were not very accessible, and Brian is drawing up a plan which will ensure that every stallholder will have a prime position. He will also include in his design a suitable open space for the demonstrations and the dancing display. We look forward to seeing the outcome of all his hard work.

line space here please

COMPETITION

Another innovation that we are introducing this year is a competition specially for children. We have produced free packets of the following seeds which are available to ~~any~~ any child who would like to contact the Secretary. One of the new ~~class~~ classes will be for the best flowers produced from the seeds. ~~A list~~ A list of the seeds available is given below for your information.

(leave 4 lines here)

COMMITTEE MEMBERS

Chairperson	J	AMOS	336529
Secretary	B	SMITH	22198
Treasurer	F	SHAW	66583
Schedules	H	FORD	98611
Entertainment	V	JAMES	66928

Graphics Assignment (solution page 130)

Handicraft entries

1 Using the Financial Statistics, create and label a pie chart showing the entries for Handicrafts for the first five years of operation.

Use the main title: Handicrafts
and the subtitle: Number of Entries

Label the segments with the years.

2 Save the display.

3 Print the display.

Collating Assignment (solution pages 131-133)

Chairperson's circular

1 Using the document produced in the word processing assignment, add the following to the text:

a From the Graphics

Either include your graphical representation after the paragraph headed Entries, or attach a copy of the diagram to the end of this document, as Appendix A *with an appropriate note in the text.*

* b From the Database

After the paragraph headed Competition insert the information on the half-hardy annuals which will grow in warm, sheltered places.

* c From the Spreadsheet

After the paragraph headed Entry Fees insert the section from the spreadsheet which shows the entry fees in all classes up to and including this year only.

2 If necessary repaginate and renumber the pages.

3 Present the final document.

Note * These items must *not be re-keyed*, but should be included by:

a using integrated software to collate the different sections;

b printing out the extracts separately from the word processed document and then sticking them in at the appropriate places; OR

c using desktop publishing facilities.

5 *College Courses*

Scenario

The department in which you are employed as a clerical assistant is expanding quickly owing to the advent of modern technology. A wide range of courses is offered, including Languages, Secretarial and National Vocational Qualifications.

The College's Academic Board meets next week, and the Head of Department has asked you to carry our certain tasks in order that information about the department may be included in a report to the Board.

Task 1 Database

Begin compiling records of student applications, using the rough lists made at interview. Obtain specific details from the records to help staff decide on individual study programmes for the students.

Task 2 Spreadsheet

Leisure courses need to be costed very carefully to make them commercially viable, but still attractive to the public. Produce a spreadsheet to help the Finance Officer fix realistic fees.

Task 3 Word Processing

Type a copy of the Head of Department's report in preparation for the next meeting of the Academic Board.

Task 4 Graphics

Produce a graph to show the number of applications to date for full-time courses.

Task 5 Collating

Complete the Departmental Head's Report, by including extracts from the database, spreadsheet and graphics tasks, where indicated.

Database Assignment (solutions pages 135-136)

Student applications

1 Using the information on the Interview and Class Lists, create a database. (You do not need the Student No.)

2 Store the data, and provide the following print-outs:

a The complete file in alphabetical order of surname.

b The names and dates of birth of everyone applying for and accepted on the Secretarial Course. Include on your print-out the course applied for and the suggested course.

c Find the records for those applicants who have applied for, and been accepted on the NVQ course, and who have one or more "O" level passes. Print the full names, and exams passed.

d The complete file in reverse alphabetical order of surname. Print the names and dates of birth only.

e The surnames and sex of those with three or more GCSEs whose suggested course is Reception. Include the suggested course and the number of GCSE passes on your print-out.

INTERVIEWS-TUESDAY.

Student No.	DoB	Sex	Course Applied For	Qualifications		
				GCSE	'O'	'A'
1	15.01.79	F	Secretarial	1	–	–
2	15.5.78	F	Reception	–	6	6
3	1.1.79	F	N.V.Q	3	–	–
4	9.6.78	F	Sec.	6	–	–
5	14.7.79	M	Rec.	0	0	0
6	6 1.77	F	Secretarial	5	1	–
7	12.12.79	F	NVQ	–	–	–
8	15 Mar 78	F	NVQ	0	4	2
9	7.12.1979	F	NVQ	3	–	0
10	5.06.78	F	Sec	–	10	3
11	17.11.77	M	NVQ	2	–	–
12	3 June 77	F	Sec.	–	5	–
13	7.7.77	F	Sec	–	6	1
14	10.9.79	F	Sec	3	0	0
15	10.10.78	M	Reception	4	1	–
16	4 Mar 79	F	NVQ	3	–	–
17	7.8.78	F	Sec.	5	–	1
18	21/5/79	M	NVQ	1	–	–
19	8/8/77	M	Rec.	3	2	–

Tuesday Interviews - Continued.

Student No.	DoB	Sex	Course Applied For	Qualifications GCSE	'O'	'A'
20	5/9/77	M	NVQ	–	5	–
21	5/6/77	F	Sec	–	5	1
22	16.02.79	F	NUQ	3	0	0
23	15 7 79	F	Reception	1	–	–
24	5 2.78	M	NUQ	1	3	~~2~~ –
25	24.7.79	F	NUQ	–	3	–
26	13.9.78	M	NUQ	–	–	4
27	2/5/79	F	Rec.	1	–	–
28	10 10 79	M	Rec	1	–	–
29	15.6.78	F	NUQ	–	1	–
30	22.2.78	F	NUQ	3	0	0
31	1 Jan 78	F	NUQ	–	1	–
32	25.12.76	F	Reception	2	–	–
33	3.9.79	F	NUQ	1	–	–

SUGGESTED CLASS GROUPS

SECRETARIAL

Student No.	Surname	Forename
2	CLARKE	Lisa
4	BAKER	Cynthia
6	HARDING	Jean
8	SCAMELL	Karen
10	JENKINS	Maureen
12	LYON	Debbie
13	BELTON	Frances
16	FREEMAN	Rachel
17	COCHRANE	Anthea
21	KITCHENER	Simone
26	DAUIS	David

N.V.Q

Student No.	SURNAME	FORENAME
3	TRUCKLE	Rosemarie
14	SMITHERS	JOANNE
18	REDSTON	Keith
19	BLESSED	Brian
20	BRINDLEY	Christopher
22	THOMPSON	Heather
24	GRAHAM	Stan
25	CHILDS	Christine
29	LIPTON	May
30	FRANCIS	Mary
31	RULE	Jennifer

RECEPTION

1	ROBERTS	Kelly
5	MCNAUGHT	Colin
7	GRANT	Jackie
9	ABBOTT	Louisa
11	FOTHERINGHAM	Tom
15	ANDREWS	Brian
23	WINGFIELD	Ivy
27	GIBSON	Stella
28	BICKER	William
32	RUCK	Maureen
33	FINN	Irene

Spreadsheet Assignment (solutions pages 137-139)

College Leisure Courses

1 Using the information given in Course Statistics, create a spreadsheet using the title Leisure Courses.

Display the figures in two sections Income and Outgoings.

Do not abbreviate subjects.

You will need a total for the number of classes held, and a total income from all sources.

After the Outgoings section include a row for Profit or Loss.

2 Enter the data.

3 Save and print the spreadsheet.

4 Print another copy of the spreadsheet showing the formulae.

5 What would be the result if the lecturers' salaries increased to £13.50 in accordance with their claim? Print the Outgoings section to show this change.

6 What difference would it make to the situation if a new class were offered? Add the following details and adjust the figures accordingly:

Photography
9 classes
12 students
Class Fee £15.00

Print the income section showing class titles, number of classes, and the total class fees only.

Course statistics

The following courses are proposed, to run for the length shown:

Course No.	*Subject*	*No. of classes*
1	Batik	20
2	Wood Turning	20
3	Fly Fishing	20
4	Upholstery	36
5	Calligraphy	36
6	Cake Decorating	36

Maximum numbers that can be accommodated for each subject are: 10 in Courses 1, 2 and 3, and 15 in all others. Assume all classes are full.

Fees:	1, 2, 4	£3.50 per class
	3	£5.00 per class
	5	£4.50 per class
	6	£8.00 per class

Students in all classes must also contribute one amount of £18.00 towards the cost of textbooks and stationery.

Running costs

All amounts are given per class:

Lecturers' salaries	£12.50
Hire of the building	£25.00
Heating/Lighting	£15.00
Caretaker's salary	£10.50

Word Processing Assignment (solution pages 140-141)

Report to Academic Board

1 Create a file using single line spacing and justified right-hand margin.

2 Enter the following text and number the pages.

3 Save and print.

Department of Business and Technology ← BOLD closed caps. @ margin

The Department provides a variety of full-time courses for those students who intend to ~~pt~~ pursue a career in Business Management or Office Administration in either the public or private sectors of industry and commerce. The business world is one that is both exciting and rapidly changing, and so the range and content of our ~~syllabus~~ courses is ~~ever~~ always being updated to ~~cope~~ meet the new demands of employers and students. Double line spacing →

Centred spaced caps all headings please

Range of Courses ←

The following table gives the complete range of courses that we shall be offering this year:

Modern Languages — Secretarial
National Vocational Qualification — Office Skills
Private Secretary's Certificate — Hotel Reception

Languages
Particular attention is drawn to the Modern Languages Course which is ~~worked~~ designed for post 'A' level students who wish to apply their language skills in a secretarial or ~~perhaps even~~ business context.

The Department is in the process of acquiring a new integrated micro-electronic language ~~labor~~ laboratory to add to its already extensive range of audio-visual equipment.

Secretarial
The Department has for ~~a long~~ some time offered a full-time, one-year course leading to the LCCI Private Secretary's Certificate. This is a prestigious course and we can only accept limited numbers – the following having been chosen so far from a short list of 30.

(leave 3 clear line spaces here)

State of the Art Equipment
The facilities of the Dept. reflect the ~~very~~ increasing influence of new technology in the office, and its importance in further and higher education courses. The typewriting rooms are fitted with the latest electronic typewriters and ~~uptodate~~ audio equipment. The ~~x~~ Training Office and Office Practice Workshop have been designed to ~~include~~ reflect modern business methods, and utilise ~~the~~ new technology, and ~~use~~ are equipped with off-set litho, fax, colour photocopying, etc.

Computing

There are now 4 (word please) micro-computing rooms with modern hardware and a variety of software for data processing and word processing, as well as for ~~use~~ use in other business studies subjects, eg Accounting & Economics, ~~Law etc~~ and for practical business simulations

Course Applications

We are pleased to see ~~report~~ that applications for next year's courses are coming in at a steady pace, and at the time of writing the position is as follows:

(leave 6 lines here please)

The Annexe Hiring

Since we moved into our new premises the old annexe has ~~been~~ unused, but this year our own Community Arts Section is proposing to ~~rent~~ hire the building for some of their leisure classes, and to put the ~~entire~~ whole scheme on ~~to~~ a ~~more~~ commercial footing. Mr Bottomley has prepared some figures giving the estimated income for the year.

(leave 4 lines here)

Perhaps we should start charging for all our classes - it certainly seems very profitable!

Graphics Assignment (solution page 142)

Applications received

1 Using the following figures create and label a chart showing the number of applications to date for the full-time courses:

Modern Languages	8
Private Secretary's Certificate	12
Hotel Reception	18
NVQ Level 1	45
NVQ Level 2	31
NVQ Level 3	15
Office Skills Refresher	15

Use the main title: Applications
For the sub-title use the current month and year.

Leave the y axis unlabelled.
Label the x axis: ML, PSC, HR, L1, L2, L3, OSR

2 Save the display.

3 Print the display.

Collating Assignment (solution pages 143-145)

Report to Academic Board

1 Using the document prepared in the word processing assignment, add the following to the text:

* a From the database

After the paragraph headed Secretarial insert the full names and dates of birth for applicants who have applied for, and been accepted, on the Secretarial Course.

b From the graphics

Insert your graphical representation after the paragraph which is headed Course Applications or attach a copy of the diagram to the end of the document, as Appendix A with an *appropriate note in the text.*

* c From the spreadsheet

In the space before the last two lines of your document insert figures and labels showing the whole of the anticipated income for the period.

2 If necessary repaginate and renumber the pages.

3 Present the final document.

Note * These items must *not be re-keyed,* but should be included by:

a Using integrated software to collate the different sections:

b Printing out the extracts separately from the word processed document and then sticking them in at the appropriate places; OR

c Using desktop publishing facilities.

6 Hotel Accommodation

Scenario

You are employed by a newly-formed company whose aim is to provide a service to companies and individuals who wish to hire hotel accommodation for conferences, weddings, etc, but who do not have time to do the searching for themselves.

Task 1 Database

In this assignment you are helping to organise data in order to provide a swift service to anyone who needs information.

Task 2 Spreadsheet

With the help of letters received from three hotels you are producing comparative figures to help a young couple decide where to hold their wedding reception.

Task 3 Word Processing

You have been asked to begin composing an advertising leaflet giving information on the type of facilities which are provided by a chain of hotels.

Task 4 Graphics

To help the couple decide on the venue for their wedding you will be producing a graph comparing the costs at the different hotels.

Task 5 Collating

In this task you will be completing the leaflet you began to compose in the Word Processing task.

Database Assignment (solutions pages 146-148)

Hotel details

1 Using the information provided on the record cards, create a database with each record containing the following information:

Hotel Name	If they cater for:	Weddings
Town		Conferences
Telephone Number		Private parties
Manager's Name	(use a two-letter code, composed of the first two letters of the word, in this field)	

Whether they can provide a full vegetarian menu
The distance from Biford

2 Save the information.

3 Print the following lists, including column headings:

a The whole file in alphabetical order of hotel name.

b The whole file in descending order of Manager's name.

c Names and telephone numbers of hotels in Burnham which can offer a full vegetarian menu.

d Find all the hotels that are less than 8 miles from Biford, and cater for weddings and private parties. Print hotel name, telephone number and Manager's name.

e The names of the hotels which can cater for Conferences.

FORDTON MANOR

TOWN. FORDTOWN TEL NO 16355
MANAGER T. KNIGHT

FUNCTIONS: Weddings ✓
Conferences ...
Private Parties ✓

Full Vegetarian Menu? X
Distance from Biford 7 miles

BURNHAM GRANGE

TOWN. BURNHAM TEL NO 36911
MANAGER A. MUGOMBA

FUNCTIONS: Weddings ✓
Conferences ✓
Private Parties ✓

Full Vegetarian Menu? ✓
Distance from Biford 12 miles

COLLEGE COURT

TOWN. LORDCOMBE TEL NO 323711
MANAGER G. BRAIN

FUNCTIONS: Weddings ✓
Conferences ...
Private Parties ✓

Full Vegetarian Menu? X
Distance from Biford 9 miles

COUNTRY HOUSE HOTEL

TOWN. MAPLEDENE TEL NO 22583
MANAGER N. CORY

FUNCTIONS: Weddings ✓
Conferences ...
Private Parties ✓

Full Vegetarian Menu? —
Distance from Biford 20 miles

BRYANSCOMBE

TOWN. FORDTOWN TEL NO 66328
MANAGER R. CANNING

FUNCTIONS: Weddings ...
Conferences ✓
Private Parties ✓

Full Vegetarian Menu? —
Distance from Biford 7 miles

BRITANNIA HOTEL

TOWN. LOWER CHERRINGTON TEL NO. 467
MANAGER J. CHESTERTON

FUNCTIONS: Weddings ✓
Conferences ...
Private Parties ...

Full Vegetarian Menu? NO
Distance from Biford 3 miles

ATHENE HOTEL

TOWN: BROUGHTON ABBEY — TEL NO: 660044
MANAGER: B.R. SUTTON

FUNCTIONS: Weddings ✓
Conferences
Private Parties ✓

Full Vegetarian Menu? ✓
Distance from Biford: 5 miles

THE BRINSMEAD

TOWN: EXETER — TEL NO: 41077
MANAGER: K. WATERHOUSE

FUNCTIONS: Weddings ✓
Conferences ✓
Private Parties ✓

Full Vegetarian Menu? NO
Distance from Biford: 7 miles

THE ACROPOLIS

TOWN: EXETER — TEL NO: 410633
MANAGER: P. ROLFS

FUNCTIONS: Weddings ✓
Conferences ✓
Private Parties ✓

Full Vegetarian Menu? ✓
Distance from Biford: 10 miles

ROBBINS HOTEL

TOWN: BURNHAM — TEL NO: 21007
MANAGER: R. BYRD

FUNCTIONS: Weddings
Conferences ✓
Private Parties ✓

Full Vegetarian Menu? Yes
Distance from Biford: 12 miles

MAPLES

TOWN: FORDTOWN — TEL NO: 660043
MANAGER: B. SMITH

FUNCTIONS: Weddings ✓
Conferences
Private Parties ✓

Full Vegetarian Menu? —
Distance from Biford: 7 miles

CANTALOUPE HOTEL

TOWN: FORDTOWN — TEL NO: 116387
MANAGER: G. FORDHAM

FUNCTIONS: Weddings ✓
Conferences ✓
Private Parties

Full Vegetarian Menu? NO
Distance from Biford: 7 miles

MOAT HOUSE

TOWN: COPPLESTONE — TEL NO: 33771
MANAGER: B. MAYNARD

FUNCTIONS: Weddings ✓
Conferences
Private Parties ✓

Full Vegetarian Menu? No
Distance from Biford: 10 miles

COUNTY

TOWN: BURNHAM — TEL NO: 113291
MANAGER: J. CROUCH

FUNCTIONS: Weddings ✓
Conferences ✓
Private Parties ✓

Full Vegetarian Menu? ✓
Distance from Biford: 12 miles

COLEBROOK HOTEL

TOWN: INCHESTER — TEL NO: 32107
MANAGER: M. NORTON

FUNCTIONS: Weddings ✓
Conferences
Private Parties ✓

Full Vegetarian Menu? ✓
Distance from Biford: 8 miles

THE ROYAL CAVALIER HOTEL

TOWN: STEEPLE UNDER WYCHWOOD — TEL NO: 667353
MANAGER: B.J. BARCLAY

FUNCTIONS: Weddings ✓
Conferences ✓
Private Parties

Full Vegetarian Menu?
Distance from Biford: 8 miles

ST. BERNARD'S ABBEY

TOWN: ST. BERNARD'S TEL NO: 22919
MANAGER: B. MONK

FUNCTIONS: Weddings
Conferences ✓
Private Parties ✓

Full Vegetarian Menu? ✓
Distance from Biford: 11 miles

COMBE HOTEL

TOWN: LORDCOMBE TEL NO: 89119
MANAGER: P. LORD

FUNCTIONS: Weddings ✓
Conferences ✓
Private Parties ✓

Full Vegetarian Menu? No.
Distance from Biford: 9 miles

TRELAWNY HOTEL

TOWN: INCHESTER TEL NO: 34690
MANAGER: J. COOKE

FUNCTIONS: Weddings ✓
Conferences
Private Parties ✓

Full Vegetarian Menu? No.
Distance from Biford: 8 miles

IVANHOE

TOWN: LORDCOMBE TEL NO: 89118
MANAGER: M. DAVIES

FUNCTIONS: Weddings
Conferences ✓
Private Parties ✓

Full Vegetarian Menu? ✓
Distance from Biford: 9 miles

WHITE HART

TOWN: MAPLEDENE TEL NO: 99160
MANAGER: D. FORTESCUE

FUNCTIONS: Weddings ✓
Conferences
Private Parties ✓

Full Vegetarian Menu? Yes
Distance from Biford: 20 miles

ABBEY HOUSE

TOWN: ST. BERNARD'S TEL NO: 29718
MANAGER: C. MEADER

FUNCTIONS: Weddings ✓
Conferences
Private Parties ✓

Full Vegetarian Menu? Yes
Distance from Biford: 11 miles

BISHOP'S LODGE

TOWN: ST. BERNARDS TEL NO: 66723
MANAGER: B. LOVELL

FUNCTIONS: Weddings ✓
Conferences ✓
Private Parties ✓

Full Vegetarian Menu? None
Distance from Biford: 11 miles

GORDON HOUSE HOTEL

TOWN: INCHESTER TEL NO: 29818
MANAGER: S. GORDON

FUNCTIONS: Weddings ✓
Conferences
Private Parties ✓

Full Vegetarian Menu? No.
Distance from Biford: 8 miles

AMBLESIDE HOTEL

TOWN: MAPLEDENE TEL NO: 43106
MANAGER: K. GREENE

FUNCTIONS: Weddings ✓
Conferences
Private Parties ✓

Full Vegetarian Menu? No.
Distance from Biford: 20 miles

LORDCOMBE MANOR

TOWN: LORDCOMBE TEL NO: 44587
MANAGER: J. ADAMS

FUNCTIONS: Weddings ✓
Conferences ✓
Private Parties ✓

Full Vegetarian Menu? ✓
Distance from Biford: 9 miles

THROOPE HOUSE

TOWN. BURNHAM . . TEL NO. 61809
MANAGER. . . R. BROOKE . . . . . .

FUNCTIONS: Weddings ✓
Conferences . .
Private Parties ✓

Full Vegetarian Menu? ✓ . . . .
Distance from Biford. 12 . . . miles

COPPLESTONE HOUSE

TOWN. COPPLESTONE TEL NO 23610
MANAGER. . H. TORRES . . . .

FUNCTIONS: Weddings ✓
Conferences ✓
Private Parties ✓

Full Vegetarian Menu? No . .
Distance from Biford. . 10 . . miles

MILLSTREAM HOTEL

TOWN COPPLESTONE TEL NO 22236
MANAGER. . J. SEDDON . . . .

FUNCTIONS: Weddings ✓
Conferences ✓
Private Parties . . .

Full Vegetarian Menu? ✓ . . . .
Distance from Biford. . 10 . . miles

RESTAWHILE

TOWN. FORDTOWN . . TEL NO 29973
MANAGER. . J. GRINTER . . . . . .

FUNCTIONS: Weddings ✓
Conferences ✓
Private Parties ✓

Full Vegetarian Menu? ✓ . . . .
Distance from Biford. 7 . . . miles

Spreadsheet Assignment (solutions pages 149-150)

Comparative costs

1 Three letters have been received from hotels giving details of the services they can offer - using this information construct a spreadsheet with the heading: Comparative Costs for Wedding. (60 guests)

2 Include all the information you have and, using a formula, produce a total for each hotel's quotation. Print out the spreadsheet.

3 Print the portion of the spreadsheet which shows the prices of wine and champagne in the three hotels.

4 The couple have been told on the telephone that costs for all hotels will rise by 3% by the end of the year. Add another row labelled 3% Increase and work out the amount of the increase. Print the rows showing the Totals and the Increase only.

5 Calculate the total costs for the function if it is delayed until the end of the year. Print a copy.

BRITANNIA HOTEL

LOWER CHERRINGTON

Manager: J Chesterton   Telephone: Cherrington 467

5 May 19..

Dear Sir

Thank you for your letter enquiring our rates for Weddings. We give below the information for which you have asked, but if you have any further queries please do not hesitate to contact us.

Room Hire to include tables, chairs, table decorations and waitress service:

Seating capacity 60 - £320

Three-tier cake - price varies depending on decoration. We shall be pleased to discuss this at your convenience. Average price £150.

Wine (per bottle) £8.00
(allow 6 glasses per bottle)
Champagne (per bottle) £29.50
(allow 6 glasses per bottle)

Full Buffet - per person - 60 people: £10.50

Coffee and mints are included in price of buffet.

We enclose our full range of menus for your consideration.

Use of private room for changing/rest room - £10.50

At the moment we are not able to offer the services of a Master of Ceremonies.

We can also arrange for our own photographer to attend and take photos of the reception and in the garden by the pool at the rate of £125.

Attached please find our fully illustrated brochure showing the delightful grounds in which the hotel is situated, and including charming shots of the dining room and reception areas. We think you will agree that our hotel is second to none when it comes to choosing a venue for that special occasion.

Yours faithfully

Manager

ATHENE HOTEL

BROUGHTON ABBEY

Manager: B R Sutton
Tel: Broughton Abbey 660044

10 May 19..

Dear Mr Cunningham

Thank you for your enquiry regarding a venue for your forthcoming wedding. We are pleased to give you the following information which we hope will help you make your choice. May we assure you of our very best attention at all times, and we hope you will telephone our Manager, Mr Sutton, if there is any other way in which we can be of assistance:

Hire of room - all inclusive: £300.

Our chef is renowned for his fabulously decorated wedding cakes, and as each one is individually designed, the cost will obviously vary, but as a guide you should allow for about £200.

Our most popular wine - "Oriantales Blanc" - £8.76 per bottle.
An excellent medium-priced champagne - £19.50 per bottle.

Our special varied buffet is £12.50 per head for 60 guests.

Coffee and mints to round off the perfect meal - 35p per person.

A rest room can be put at your disposal for no extra charge and a Master of Ceremonies can preside at the occasion for only £50.

If you wish us to arrange a photographer, Mr Carl Ruben of Broughton Abbey is always delighted to attend functions and his charge is only £180. The cost of photographs is, of course, additional.

We have great pleasure in enclosing our fully-comprehensive literature which gives much more complete information about all the services we can offer, and, when you have had an opportunity to peruse this, we shall be very pleased to arrange a meeting with our Manager in order to discuss any queries you may have.

Yours sincerely

Catering Manager

The Royal Cavalier Hotel

Steeple Under Wychwood Tel: S.U.W. 667353

==

Manager: B J Barclay

==

3 May 19..

Dear Sir

We have received your letter regarding your forthcoming marriage and are pleased to give the following information in answer to your questions. May we bring to your attention that the figures are only approximate, but that if you need firmer information our Banqueting Manager will be pleased to discuss these with you.

Buffet (per person)	£15
Champagne (per bottle - 6 glasses average)	£37.50
Wine (per bottle - 6 glasses average)	£9.75
Room - including tabling, seating etc	£500
3-tier wedding cake - average price	£250
Coffee (per person)	£0.75
Use of rest room/changing room	£60
Photographer	£100
Waiters (each) (one for every 10 guests)	£15
Master of Ceremonies	£50

We do hope these figures meet with your approval, and will help you in coming to a decision and we look forward to hearing from you again, when we can discuss your requirements in more detail.

Thank you for your enquiry.

Yours faithfully

Manager

Word Processing Assignment (solutions pages 151-152)

Advertising leaflet

1 Create a file using single line spacing and an unjustified right margin.

2 Enter the following text and number the pages at the foot in the centre of the page.

3 Save and print.

THE OTTERBURN HOTEL GROUP → Centre (Please use a larger font)

The Otterburn group is dedicated to providing high-quality accommodation for the discerning traveller at reasonable prices. Our hotels are all luxuriously equipped & are situated in the most desirable positions, both in city centres & the countryside. [Bold please & double spacing]

The three newest hotels in the group were / all opened only last year and maintain the high quality which the public has come to expect from Otterburn.

Britannia Hotel Lower Charrington
The Acropolis Exeter
Royal Edinburgh Edinburgh

You will be assured of a friendly welcome & excellent food in our restaurants which are an important part of all hotels. An exciting innovation at all our restaurants is the introduction of a full vegetarian menu which is available at all times; both for your enjoyment at a family ~~occasion~~ meal, or for a conference or wedding celebration. Details of the hotels in your area are given below.

↓ leave 1"

The bedrooms are all spacious double or twin rooms, including a number of suites, family, non-smoking and lady Rooms, as well as rooms designed (2) specifically (1) for disabled ~~persons~~ guests. All have the range of facilities you would expect from hotels of this standard - including remote-controlled television with in-house movies, radio, direct dial telephone, trouser press, hairdryer, beverage tray & / the optional 24-hour Room Service.

No doubt you will require a first-class wine to serve ~~to~~ at your function, & we give below wine & champagne costs for your information.

↕ (leave remainder of page blank)

For couples ~~who~~ wishing to book accommodation for the perfect Reception, our facilities are second to none. An idea of the total cost of such an occasion is given below, & we think you will agree that our rates are very competitive.

→ leave 1"

At the heart of all our hotels lies The ~~Atrium~~ TROPICANA – a glass-roofed, climate-controlled leisure club. Pools, palm-trees, the Coffee Bar & relaxation area, together with the warm climate, create a tropical environment. Whatever the season ~~is~~ outside, you can relax & recover from a hectic day's business or sight-seeing by lounging in sub-tropical temperatures.

To complete the scene, our Leisure Club has high-powered sunbeds to provide a fast tan, enabling you to return home looking, as well as feeling, great.

All our hotels boast:

* a fully equipped gymnasium
* sauna
* steamroom
* whirlpool
* cold plunge pool
* swimming pool

and everything is at your disposal, as our guest.

Our fully trained leisure staff are available to assist & advise at all times.

Graphics Assignment (solution page 153)

Comparison of charges

1 Using the information in the spreadsheet create and label a chart showing the total costs charged by each hotel if the wedding takes place before the end of the year.

Insert a main title: Reception Costs

Label the x-axis with the hotel names, or suitable abbreviations, and label the y-axis £ Sterling.

2 Save the display.

3 Print the display.

Collating Assignment (solution pages 154-156)

Advertising leaflet

1 Using the document which you prepared for the Word Processing Assignment, add the following information to the text:

* 2 From the database

Before the paragraph which begins "The bedrooms are all spacious..." insert the extract from the database which shows hotels which can cater for conferences.

* 3 From the spreadsheet

After the paragraph beginning "No doubt you will require. . ." insert the extract which shows wine and champagne costs for the three hotels.

4 From the graphics

Insert your graphical representation after the paragraph which begins "For couples wishing . . ."

5 If necessary, repaginate and renumber the pages.

6 Present the final document.

Note * These items must *not be re-keyed,* but should be included by:

a using integrated software to collate the different sections;

b printing out the extracts separately from the word processed document and then sticking them in at the appropriate places; OR

c using desktop publishing facilities.

7 Solutions to Assignments

The Little Theatre

Database Solutions

Question 3a
(The database consists of 33 records)

SURNAME	FORENAME	SEX	INTEREST	PREFERENCE	TEL NO	CAR
ACLAND	HILARY	F	CA	M	57891	YES
ADAMS	MONICA	F	MU	C	-	NO
BELLINGER	BERNARD	M	AC	C	6630	YES
BERTRAM	ADELE	F	LI	S	23611	NO
BRITAIN	BERYL	F	PR	C	23711	NO
CHURCHMAN	CHARLES	M	GN	C	9506	NO
COOMBS	ANDREW	M	GN	M	21484	YES
FOGARTY	MAXINE	F	SM	M	36428	YES
FOSDIKE	BERT	M	AC	C	99932	YES
FRIEND	ALAN	M	AC	S	EX-DIR	YES
FROOL	RAYMOND	M	FH	D	3336	NO
GASPARD	RENE	M	SM	D	60603	YES
GOLDING	MARTIN	M	AC	S	3610	YES
GRANT	FREDA	F	MU	D	63029	YES
GREGORY	LANCE	M	AC	M	-	NO
JENNINGS	JOHN	M	MU	M	339712	YES
JONES	RAY	M	CA	D	39210	NO
KITCHENER	KATE	F	MU	C	66663	NO
LITTLE	FRANCES	F	SM	C	8832	YES
MARTIN	MARGARET	F	PR	D	44812	NO
MARTIN	JANET	F	AC	S	-	YES
PRINCE	CHRISTOPHER	M	AC	M	98711	YES
PRITCHARD	KAREN	F	CA	C	4482	NO
ROBBINS	MATTHEW	M	GN	S	21088	NO
ROBBINS	PHILIP	M	GN	S	21088	NO
ROYAL	BERNARD	M	FH	S	8772	NO
SMITHSON	JEANNIE	F	PR	D	268115	YES
SPUMANTI	CARMEN	F	LI	M	EX-DIR	NO
TALESMAN	CAROLE	F	FH	S	55560	YES
THOMAS	JILL	F	PR	C	32019	YES
VARCOE	SHEILA	F	MU	D	6811	YES
WOODWARD	EDWIN	M	AC	S	5560	YES
YOGGI	MAX	M	FH	S	6444	NO

Question 3b

SURNAME	FORENAME	TEL NO
BERTRAM	ADELE	23611
MARTIN	JANET	-
TALESMAN	CAROLE	55560

Question 3c

SURNAME	FORENAME	SEX	INTEREST	PREF	TEL NO	CAR
FROOL	RAYMOND	M	FH	D	3336	NO
ROYAL	BERNARD	M	FH	S	8772	NO
YOGGI	MAX	M	FH	S	6444	NO

Question 3d

SURNAME	FORENAME	SEX	TEL NO
FOGARTY	MAXINE	F	36428
GASPARD	RENE	M	60603
LITTLE	FRANCES	F	8832

Question 3e

SURNAME	FORENAME
BELLINGER	BERNARD
FOSDIKE	BERT

Question 3f

SURNAME	FORENAME	SEX	INTEREST	PREF	TEL NO	CAR
FOGARTY	MAXINE	F	SM	M	36428	YES
GASPARD	RENE	M	SM	D	60603	YES
LITTLE	FRANCES	F	SM	C	8832	YES
SMITHSON	JEANNIE	F	PR	D	268115	YES
THOMAS	JILL	F	PR	C	32019	YES

Spreadsheet Solutions

Question 4

The Little Theatre - Production Statistics

INCOME				
Seat sales	Prod 1	Prod 2	Prod 3	Prod 4
Seat cost	2.50	2.75	2.75	2.50
No sold	70	120	200	95
Sub total	175.00	330.00	550.00	237.50
Bar	40.56	135.00	350.96	38.44
Programmes	7.00	9.50	19.60	20.40
Sub total	47.56	144.50	370.56	58.84
Total	222.56	474.50	920.56	296.34
EXPENSES				
Print/Adv	35.00	35.88	36.77	37.69
Heat/Light	30.00	30.00	30.00	30.00
Bar	45.38	45.38	45.38	45.38
Props	34.75	0.00	0.00	56.00
Royalties	70.00	70.00	70.00	0.00
Costumes	12.75	25.50	224.12	156.80
Total costs per production	227.88	206.76	406.27	325.87
Profit/Loss	-5.32	267.75	514.29	-29.53

	Adults	Children	Total
Stage Management	3	0	3
Production	2	0	2
Acting	34	15	49
Scenery	25	3	28
Front of House	15	0	15
Box Office	5	0	5
Refreshments	0	6	6

Question 4 - Formulae

The Little Theatre - - Production Statistics

INCOME				
Seat sales	Prod 1	Prod 2	Prod 3	Prod 4
Seat cost	2.5	2.75	2.75	2.5
No sold	70	120	200	95
Sub total	=+C7*C8	=+D7*D8	=+E7*E8	=+F7*F8
Bar	40.56	135	350.96	38.44
Programmes	7	9.5	19.6	20.4
Sub total	=+C13+C14	=+D13+D14	=+E13+E14	=+F13+F14
Total	=+C16+C10	=+D16+D10	=+E16+E10	=+F16+F10
EXPENSES				
Print/Adv	35	=+C22+C22*0.025	=+D22+D22*0.025	=+E22+E22*0.025
Heat/Light	30	30	30	30
Bar	45.38	45.38	45.38	45.38
Props	34.75	0	0	56
Royalties	70	70	70	0
Costumes	12.75	25.5	224.12	156.8
Total costs per production	=SUM(C22:C27)	=SUM(D22:D27)	=SUM(E22:E27)	=SUM(F22:F27)
Profit/Loss	=+C18-C30	=+D18-D30	=+E18-E30	=+F18-F30
	Adults	Children	Total	
Stage Management	3	0	=+C36+D36	
Production	2	0	=+C37+D37	
Acting	34	15	=+C38+D38	
Scenery	25	3	=+C39+D39	
Front of House	15	0	=+C40+D40	
Box Office	5	0	=+C41+D41	
Refreshments	0	6	=+C42+D42	

Question 5

The Little Theatre - Production Statistics

INCOME				
Seat sales	Prod 1	Prod 2	Prod 3	Prod 4
Seat cost	2.50	2.75	2.75	2.50
No Sold	70	120	200	95
Sub total	175.00	330.00	550.00	237.50
Bar	40.56	135.00	350.96	38.44
Programmes	7.00	9.50	19.60	20.40
Sub total	47.56	144.50	370.56	58.84
Total	222.56	474.50	920.56	296.34
EXPENSES				
Print/Adv	35.00	35.88	36.77	37.69
Heat/Light	30.00	30.00	30.00	30.00
Bar	45.38	45.38	45.38	45.38
Props	34.75	0.00	0.00	56.00
Royalties	70.00	70.00	70.00	0.00
Costumes	12.75	25.50	224.12	156.80
Scripts	15.58	15.58	15.58	15.58
Total costs per production	243.46	222.34	421.85	341.45
Profit/Loss	-20.90	252.16	498.71	-45.11

	Adults	Children	Total
Stage Management	3	0	3
Production	2	0	2
Acting	34	15	49
Scenery	25	3	28
Front of House	15	0	15
Box Office	5	0	5
Refreshments	0	6	6

Question 6

The Little Theatre - Production Statistics

INCOME

Seat sales	Prod 1	Prod 2	Prod 3	Prod 4
Seat cost	2.75	2.75	2.75	2.75
No sold	70	120	200	95
Sub total	192.50	330.00	550.00	261.25
Bar	40.56	135.00	350.96	38.44
Programmes	7.00	9.50	19.60	20.40
Sub total	47.56	144.50	370.56	58.84
Total	240.06	474.50	920.56	320.09

EXPENSES

Print/Adv	35.00	35.88	36.77	37.69
Heat/Light	30.00	30.00	30.00	30.00
Bar	45.38	45.38	45.38	45.38
Props	34.75	0.00	0.00	56.00
Royalties	70.00	70.00	70.00	0.00
Costumes	12.75	25.50	224.12	156.80
Scripts	15.58	15.58	15.58	15.58
Total costs per production	243.46	222.34	421.85	341.45
Profit/Loss	-3.40	252.16	498.71	-21.36

	Adults	Children	Total
Stage Management	3	0	3
Production	2	0	2
Acting	34	15	49
Scenery	25	3	28
Front of House	15	0	15
Box Office	5	0	5
Refreshments	0	6	6

Word Processing Solution

T H E   L I T T L E   T H E A T R E

The Little Theatre was started ten years ago and has gone from strength to strength. We aim to stage a variety of productions including comedy, tragedy, farce, musicals, revues and pantomime.

We have been extremely fortunate in the past year to have obtained our own premises - and what a difference it makes! Instead of having to transport scenery, lighting, costumes, etc, everything is located in one place. Absolute luxury, and we are still revelling in it!

Of course, there have been problems associated with the acquisition, the main one being finance. The hall we have purchased (or, to be more accurate, are purchasing with a mortgage) cost £5,000, of which we were able to put £2,000 as a deposit, which leaves us still with a considerable amount to find. However, with determination and hard work, we are confident that we can repay the loan within the next five years.

THE PLAYS

This year we have staged the following productions:

Mother Courage	See How They Run
Anne Frank	The Tempest

Two made a loss, one a slight profit, and the other a gratifyingly large profit. This is very encouraging, but we must not "rest on our laurels" - rather the opposite - and must go forward determined to do even better.

When we look for reasons to explain the losses made on the two productions, it is obvious that we did not sell enough tickets, and members are urged to maintain their efforts to publicise productions and sell as many tickets as possible. Please do your best - remember, we depend on ticket sales as our main source of income.

1

When members first join, we do, of course, like to find out their own particular interest, whether it be acting, front of house, scenery painting, lighting, etc. However, when a play is in production, everyone is expected (and is usually very willing) to turn a hand to anything.

Thus we have the situation, as we did recently, where one of our members was ably taking the lead in "Mother Courage", but in the next production was in charge of interval refreshments. This way we find makes for good feeling and a sense of fairness all round.

SKILLS

At any one time there are a number of people who can be called upon to help in all sections - but as the following graph shows, the numbers offering to help with Stage Management and Production are very low.

A PLEA

These jobs are a little more specialised, of course, but we would be very pleased if all members could give the matter some careful consideration. If you would be willing to help with any of these jobs perhaps you would like to contact one of the following, who will arrange for you to work alongside him/her learning the intricacies of the job.

Graphics Solution

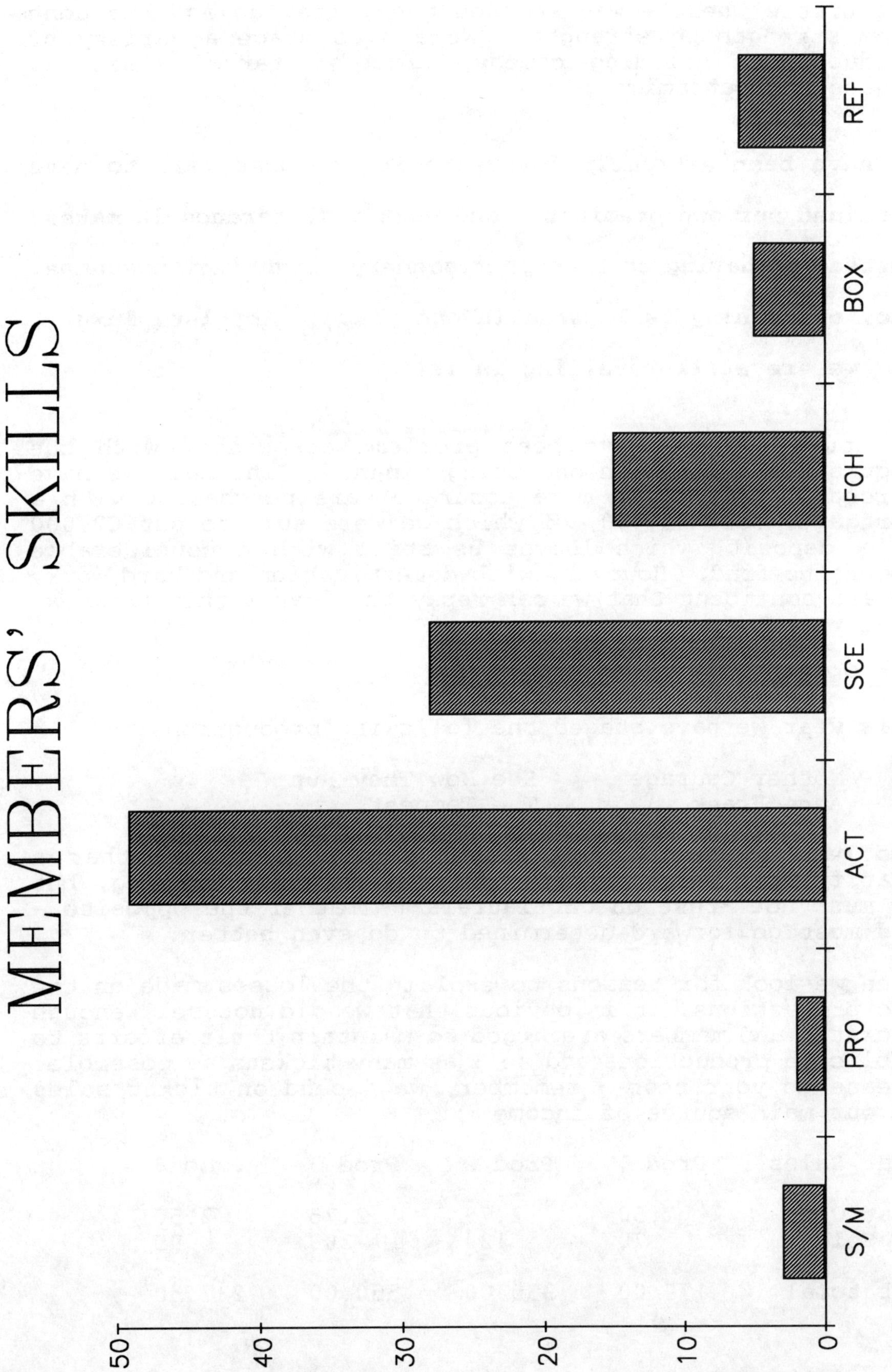

Collating Solution

T H E   L I T T L E   T H E A T R E

The Little Theatre was started ten years ago and has gone from strength to strength. We aim to stage a variety of productions including comedy, tragedy, farce, musicals, revues and pantomime.

We have been extremely fortunate in the past year to have obtained our own premises - and what a difference it makes! Instead of having to transport scenery, lighting, costumes, etc, everything is located in one place. Absolute luxury, and we are still revelling in it!

Of course, there have been problems associated with the acquisition, the main one being finance. The hall we have purchased (or, to be more accurate, are purchasing with a mortgage) cost £5,000, of which we were able to put £2,000 as a deposit, which leaves us still with a considerable amount to find. However, with determination and hard work, we are confident that we can repay the loan within the next five years.

THE PLAYS

This year we have staged the following productions:

Mother Courage	See How They Run
Anne Frank	The Tempest

Two made a loss, one a slight profit, and the other a gratifyingly large profit. This is very encouraging, but we must not "rest on our laurels" - rather the opposite - and must go forward determined to do even better.

When we look for reasons to explain the losses made on the two productions, it is obvious that we did not sell enough tickets, and members are urged to maintain their efforts to publicise productions and sell as many tickets as possible. Please do your best - remember, we depend on ticket sales as our main source of income.

Seat Sales	Prod 1	Prod 2	Prod 3	Prod 4
Seat Cost	2.50	2.75	2.75	2.50
No Sold	70	120	200	95
Sub total	175.00	330.00	550.00	237.50

1

When members first join, we do, of course, like to find out their own particular interest, whether it be acting, front of house, scenery painting, lighting, etc. However, when a play is in production, everyone is expected (and is usually very willing) to turn a hand to anything.

Thus we have the situation, as we did recently, where one of our members was ably taking the lead in "Mother Courage", but in the next production was in charge of interval refreshments. This way we find makes for good feeling and a sense of fairness all round.

<u>SKILLS</u>

At any one time there are a number of people who can be called upon to help in all sections - but as the following graph shows, the numbers offering to help with Stage Management and Production are very low.

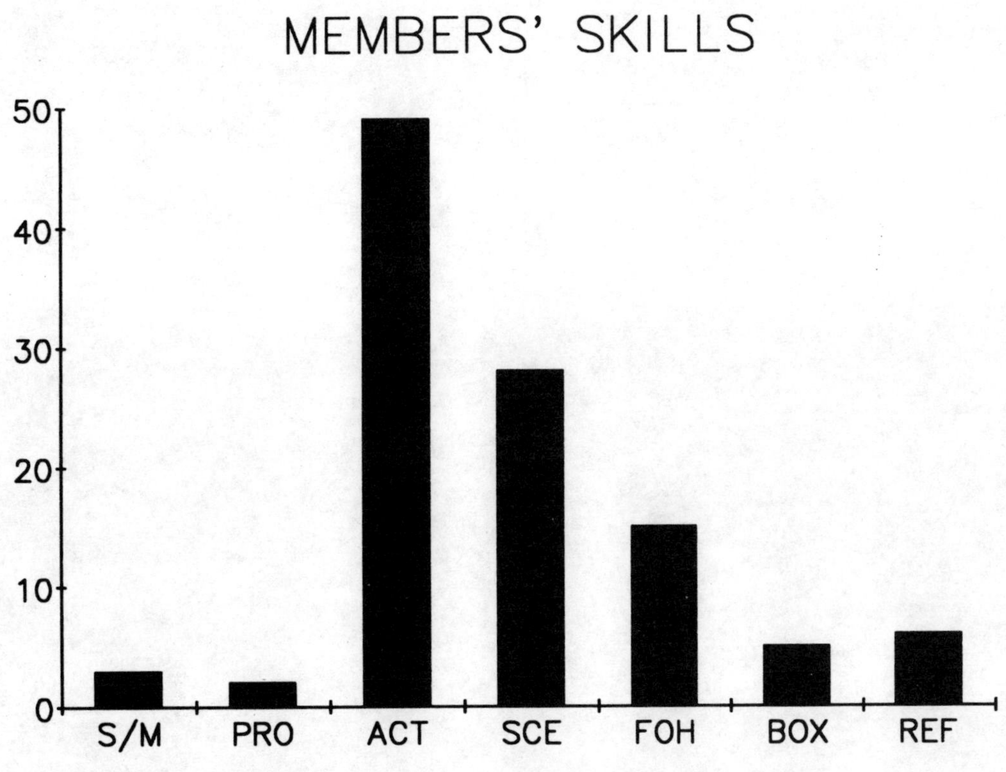

2

A PLEA

These jobs are a little more specialised, of course, but we would be very pleased if all members could give the matter some careful consideration. If you would be willing to help with any of these jobs perhaps you would like to contact one of the following, who will arrange for you to work alongside him/her learning the intricacies of the job.

SURNAME	FORENAME	INTEREST	TEL NO
FOGARTY	MAXINE	SM	36428
GASPARD	RENE	SM	60603
LITTLE	FRANCES	SM	8832
SMITHSON	JEANNIE	PR	268115
THOMAS	JILL	PR	32019

3

Health and Fitness Club

Database Solutions

Question 2
(The database consists of 33 records)

SURNAME	FORENAME	ADDRESS	TOWN	SEX	DoB	CAT	INTEREST
BASCHE	BEV	TREE TOPS	DURRINGTON	F	15.06.46	A	SQUASH
BENTLEY	MAUREEN	THE BEECHES	WILTON	F	25.12.68	YA	SQUASH
BEST	AMANDA	26 THE MILL	DURRINGTON	F	06.12.43	A	SAUNA
BRIANT	RACHEL	7 SUSSEX SQUARE	DURRINGTON	F	03.01.71	YA	GYM
CARDING	MATTHEW	106 FAR ROAD	WILTON	M	10.06.76	J	GYM
CHRISTIE	CHRISTINE	36 DURYARD	DURRINGTON	F	16.12.70	YA	SAUNA
CURTIS	DAVID	26 HIGH RISE	WILTON	M	15.10.60	A	SAUNA
DAVIS	SIMON	22 GAS LANE	WILTON	M	15.09.77	J	GYM
ENGLISH	SUE	21 MARY HOLLOW	DURRINGTON	F	03.06.78	J	GYM
FORMAN	DAVID	17 KITE STREET	SALISBURY	M	15.03.73	J	GYM
FRIEND	JO	19 HIGH RISE	WILTON	F	11.06.68	YA	SAUNA
GREGORY	FREDERICK	126 FISH ROW	SALISBURY	M	24.07.38	A	SNOOKER
HESSAYON	GEORGE	15 BROWN CLOSE	SALISBURY	M	13.06.40	A	GYM
HOLLAND	PAULINE	11 MARY HOLLOW	DURRINGTON	F	15.02.70	YA	GYM
IRONSIDE	PAUL	47 THE CUTTING	SALISBURY	M	15.07.76	YA	GYM
JONES	CHRISTOPHER	15 MILL GARDENS	WILTON	M	23.07.59	A	SQUASH
KING	LOUISE	15 KITE STREET	SALISBURY	F	10.05.73	J	GYM
KIRK	BRIAN	10 FISH ROW	SALISBURY	M	13.09.37	A	SNOOKER
MANNING	BARBARA	26 BARNABY ROAD	SALISBURY	F	13.12.50	A	SQUASH
MANNING	ALAN	26 BARNABY ROAD	SALISBURY	M	02.06.48	A	SQUASH
MICHAELS	JANET	12 RED BANK	WILTON	F	03.03.45	A	SAUNA
MOLINEAU	BARBARA	263 FAR ROAD	WILTON	F	12.03.63	YA	SAUNA
POINTER	ELIZABETH	90 SUNSET DRIVE	DURRINGTON	F	26.06.71	YA	GYM
SALISBURY	MICHAEL	15 FISH ROW	WILTON	M	10.10.64	YA	SQUASH
SIMMONDS	ANNE	10 THE MILL	DURRINGTON	F	03.10.70	YA	SQUASH
SMITH	WALTER	?		M	12.08.50	A	SNOOKER
SMITH	ANNE	?		F	?	YA	SNOOKER
SMITH	HAROLD	?		M	?	A	SNOOKER
THOMAS	THOMAS	15 DURYARD	DURRINGTON	M	19.06.65	YA	SAUNA
THOMPSON	BRENDA	26 DEVON ROAD	WILTON	F	30.12.60	A	SNOOKER
THOMPSON	PHILLIP	26 DEVON ROAD	WILTON	M	30.11.59	A	SQUASH
WELDON	FRANCIS	10 THE MILL	DURRINGTON	M	03.08.76	J	GYM
WORT	CHRIS	15 THE TERRACE	SALISBURY	M	02.02.50	A	SQUASH

Question 3a

SURNAME	FORENAME	CAT
GREGORY	FREDERICK	A
KIRK	BRIAN	A
SMITH	WALTER	A
SMITH	ANNE	YA
SMITH	HAROLD	A
THOMPSON	BRENDA	A

Question 3b

SURNAME	ADDRESS	TOWN	DoB
BRIANT	7 SUSSEX SQUARE	DURRINGTON	03.01.71
HOLLAND	11 MARY HOLLOW	DURRINGTON	15.02.70
POINTER	90 SUNSET DRIVE	DURRINGTON	26.06.71

Question 3c

SURNAME	FORENAME	CAT	INTEREST
SMITH	WALTER	A	SNOOKER
SMITH	ANNE	YA	SNOOKER
SMITH	HAROLD	A	SNOOKER

Spreadsheet Solutions

Question 2

Health and Fitness Club - Financial Statistics (Year 1)

Income

Annual subscriptions	No. of members	Annual fees	Annual receipts
Adult	350	115.00	40250.00
Young Adult	120	70.00	8400.00
Junior	50	30.00	1500.00
Total Subs			50150.00

Squash Court and Gymnasium	Fees per session	No. of sessions daily	No. of sessions weekly	Weekly takings	
Adult	2.05		263	538.13	
Young Adult	1.75		90	157.50	
Juniors	1.10		38	41.25	
				736.88	38317.50
Snooker Table	3.50	5	35	122.50	6370.00
Sauna					
No. of people					
5	2.05	15	105	1076.25	55965.00
Bar/Restaurant	500.00	1	7	3500.00	182000.00
Total Income					332802.50

Expenditure	No. of Staff	Weekly Pay	Total Weekly	
Specialists	25	200.00	5000.00	260000.00
Cleaners	5	50.00	250.00	13000.00
Overheads			1000.00	52000.00
Total Overheads				325000.00
Profit/Loss				7802.50

(NOTE: The number of sessions weekly for Juniors using the Squash Court and Gymnasium, is actually 37.5. However, bookings are per session, therefore the figure must be rounded up to 38. The total will remain at 41.25 unless the 38 is keyed in manually, which will then affect the remaining figures).

Question 3a

Squash Court and Gymnasium	Fees per session	Weekly takings
Adult	2.05	538.13
Young Adult	1.75	157.50
Juniors	1.10	41.25
		736.88
Snooker Table	3.50	122.50
Sauna		
No. of people		
5	2.05	1076.25

Question 3b

Health and Fitness Club

Income

Annual subscriptions	No. of members	Annual fees	Annual receipts
Adult	385	115.00	44275.00
Young Adult	132	70.00	9240.00
Junior	55	30.00	1650.00
Total Subs			55165.00

Squash Court and Gymnasium	Fees per session	No. of sessions daily	No. of sessions weekly	Weekly takings	
Adult	2.05		289	591.94	
Young Adult	1.75		99	173.25	
Juniors	1.10		41	45.38	
				810.56	42149.25
Snooker Table	3.50	5	35	122.50	6370.00
Sauna No. of people					
5	2.05	15	105	1076.25	55965.00
Bar/Restaurant	500.00	1	7	3500.00	182000.00
Total Income					341649.25

Expenditure	No. of Staff	Weekly Pay	Total Weekly	
Specialists	25	200.00	5000.00	260000.00
Cleaners	5	50.00	250.00	13000.00
Overheads			1000.00	52000.00
Total Overheads				325000.00
Profit/Loss				16649.25

Question 3c

Health and Fitness Club

Income

Annual subscriptions		No. of members	Annual fees		Annual receipts
Adult		385	115.00		44275.00
Young Adult		132	70.00		9240.00
Junior		55	30.00		1650.00
Total Subs					55165.00
Squash Court and Gymnasium	Fees per session	No. of sessions daily	No. of sessions weekly	Weekly takings	
Adult	2.25		289	649.69	
Young Adult	1.95		99	193.05	
Juniors	1.30		41	53.63	
				896.36	46610.85
Snooker Table	3.70	5	35	129.50	6734.00
Sauna No. of people 5	2.25	15	105	1181.25	61425.00
Bar/Restaurant	500.00	1	7	3500.00	182000.00
Total Income					351934.85
Expenditure		No. of Staff	Weekly Pay	Total Weekly	
Specialists		25	200.00	5000.00	260000.00
Cleaners		5	50.00	250.00	13000.00
Overheads				1000.00	52000.00
Total Overheads					325000.00
Profit/Loss					26934.85

Question 3d

Health and Fitness Club

Income

Annual subscriptions		No. of members	Annual fees		Annual receipts
Adult		385	115.00		44275.00
Young Adult		132	70.00		9240.00
Junior		55	30.00		1650.00
Total Subs					55165.00

Squash Court and Gymnasium	Fees per session	No. of sessions daily	No. of sessions weekly	Weekly takings	
Adult	2.25		289	649.69	
Young Adult	1.95		99	193.05	
Juniors	1.30		41	53.63	
				896.36	46610.85
Snooker Table	3.70	5	35	129.50	6734.00
Sauna					
No. of people					
5	2.25	15	105	1181.25	61425.00
Bar/Restaurant	500.00	1	7	3500.00	182000.00
Swimming Pool	2.00		572	1144	59488.00
Total Income					411422.85

Expenditure		No. of Staff	Weekly Pay	Total Weekly	
Specialists		25	200.00	5000.00	260000.00
Cleaners		5	50.00	250.00	13000.00
Overheads				1000.00	52000.00
Total Overheads					325000.00
Profit/Loss					86422.85

Question 4

Health and Fitness Club					
Income					
Annual subscriptions		No. of members	Annual fees		Annual receipts
Adult		=+350+350*0.1	115		=C8*D8
Young Adult		=+120+120*0.1	70		=C9*D9
Junior		=+50+50*0.1	30		=C10*D10
Total Subs					=SUM(F8:F10)
Squash Courts and Gymnasium	Fees per session	No. of sessions daily	No. of sessions weekly	Weekly takings	
Adult	2.25		289	=+B17*D17	
Young Adult	1.95		103	=+B18*D18	
Junior	1.3		41	=+B19*D19	
				=SUM(E17:E19)	=+E21*52
Snooker Table	3.7	5	35	=B23*D23	=E23*52
Sauna					
No. of people					
5	2.25	15	105	=B27*D27*A27	=E27*52
Swimming Pool	2		=+C8+C9+C10	=+B28*D28	=+E28*52
Bar/Restaurant	500	1	7	=B29*D29	=E29*52
Total Income					=SUM(F12:F30)
Expenditure		No. of staff	Weekly pay	Total weekly	
Specialists		25	200	=C36*D36	=E36*52
Cleaners		5	50	=C37*D37	=E37*52
Overheads				1000	=E38*52
Total Overheads					=SUM(F36:F38)
Profit/Loss					=F31-F40

Word Processing Solution

Health and Fitness Club

Newsletter

The Health and Fitness Club offers a superior gymnasium and excellent facilities for indoor leisure activities. Since the recent fire, the Club has been substantially improved to meet the recreational needs of the next decade.

Squash, snooker and pool are among the sports played at the Club. In addition there is a superb training gymnasium with fitness circuitry equipment and exercise cycles, plus a sauna.

The Club is situated in an ideal location, close to main roads, with plentiful car parking. It is housed in an architecturally pleasing building by one of the city's picturesque rivers.

The Club is open from 9.00 am to 11 pm, seven days a week.

Charges

Charges for facilities are detailed below:

Facilities

Squash Courts	Gymnasium	Sauna
Snooker Room	Sports Shop	Licensed Bar
Lounge	Coaching	Riverside Restaurant

Five Squash Courts

All courts are constructed to the highest standards including sprung beechwood floors. Tuition and coaching is provided by two approved professional coaches.

Gymnasium

The Gymnasium incorporates the latest exercise and fitness equipment in a well laid out environment with a view overlooking the river.

1

Sauna

A splendid 12-person Nordic sauna is available for the ultimate in health-promoting relaxation, together with its own shower immediately adjacent.

Snooker Room

A full-size championship snooker and billiards table provides members with a relaxing alternative to more strenuous exercise.

Our **Sports Shop** stocks a generous range of sports equipment, and advice on rackets and specialist equipment is always available.

The **Licensed Bar** is large and centrally positioned. It is open throughout the day with coffee and soft drinks always available. A varied menu is on offer in our newly completed **Restaurant** area, much of the food being homemade.

The **Lounge** adjoins the bar and provides comfortable seating with views over the garden and river. There is a small television area and daily papers and current sporting periodicals are available for members' use.

STOP PRESS

Since the fire we have managed to reorganise most of our paperwork, but the Management would be grateful if the following people could contact them as soon as possible.

2

Graphics Solution

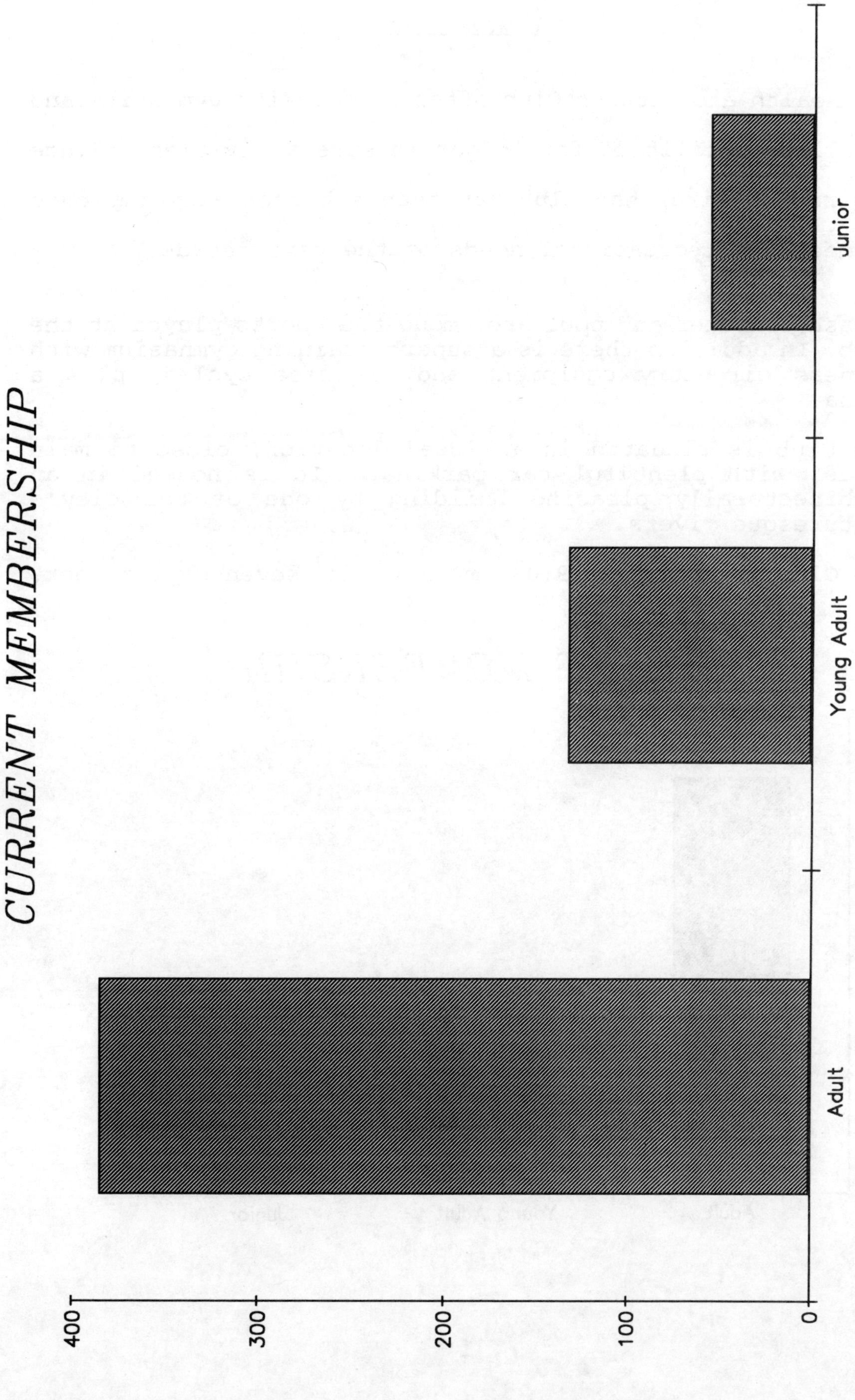

Collating Solution

Health and Fitness Club

Newsletter

The Health and Fitness Club offers a superior gymnasium and excellent facilities for indoor leisure activities. Since the recent fire, the Club has been substantially improved to meet the recreational needs of the next decade.

Squash, snooker and pool are among the sports played at the Club. In addition there is a superb training gymnasium with fitness circuitry equipment and exercise cycles, plus a sauna.

The Club is situated in an ideal location, close to main roads, with plentiful car parking. It is housed in an architecturally pleasing building by one of the city's picturesque rivers.

The Club is open from 9.00 am to 11 pm, seven days a week.

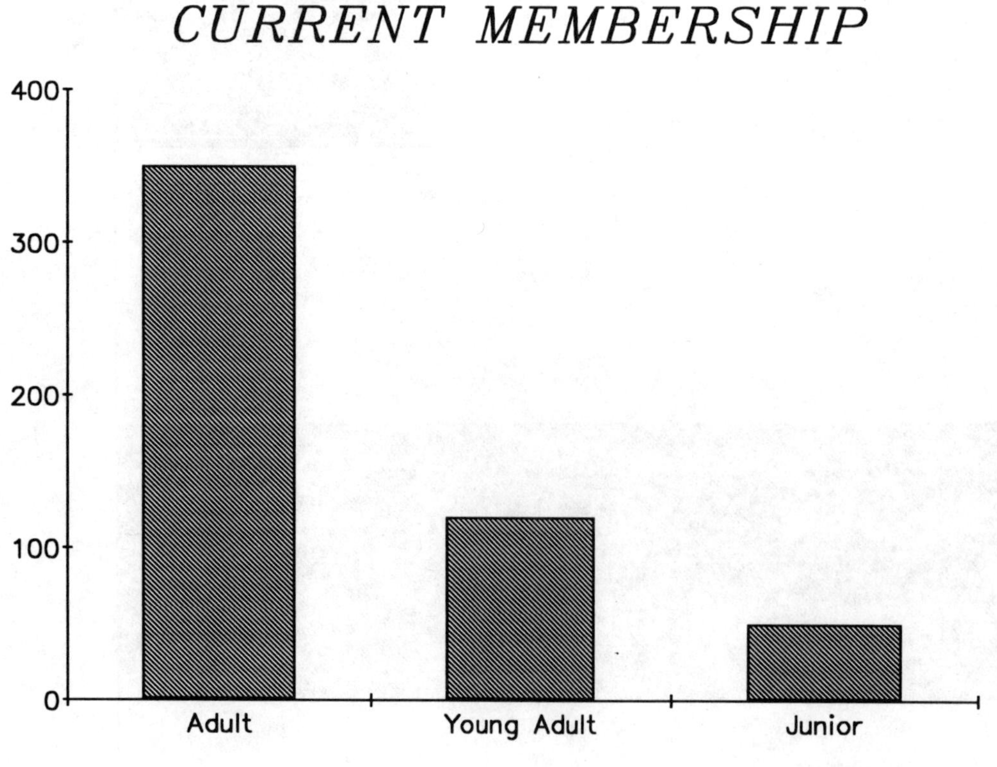

1

Charges

Charges for facilities are detailed below:

Squash Courts and Gymnasium	Fees per session
Adult	2.05
Young Adult	1.75
Junior	1.10
Snooker Table	3.50
Sauna	
No. of people	
5	2.05

Facilities

Squash Courts	Gymnasium	Sauna
Snooker Room	Sports Shop	Licensed Bar
Lounge	Coaching	Riverside Restaurant

Five Squash Courts

All courts are constructed to the highest standards including sprung beechwood floors. Tuition and coaching is provided by two approved professional coaches.

Gymnasium

The Gymnasium incorporates the latest exercise and fitness equipment in a well laid out environment with a view overlooking the river.

Sauna

A splendid 12-person Nordic sauna is available for the ultimate in health-promoting relaxation, together with its own shower immediately adjacent.

Snooker Room

A full-size championship snooker and billiards table provides members with a relaxing alternative to more strenuous exercise.

Our **Sports Shop** stocks a generous range of sports equipment, and advice on rackets and specialist equipment is always available.

2

The **Licensed Bar** is large and centrally positioned. It is open throughout the day with coffee and soft drinks always available. A varied menu is on offer in our newly completed **Restaurant** area, much of the food being homemade.

The **Lounge** adjoins the bar and provides comfortable seating with views over the garden and river. There is a small television area and daily papers and current sporting periodicals are available for members' use.

STOP PRESS

Since the fire we have managed to reorganise most of our paperwork, but the Management would be grateful if the following people could contact them as soon as possible.

FORENAME	SURNAME	CAT	INTEREST
HAROLD	SMITH	A	SNOOKER
ANNE	SMITH	YA	SNOOKER
WALTER	SMITH	A	SNOOKER

3

Publishing Company

Database Solutions

Question 3

(The database consists of 29 records)

REF NO	TITLE	AUTHOR	PUB.	CAT.	COST
T-234760	TOO MANY COOKS	BAKE	1993	TR	£12.50
E-339211	HOW TO GET ON AT MATHS	ENTWHISTLE	1993	ED	£10.99
T-234339	THREE MILES DOWN	DEEPING	1994	TR	£12.50
N-100662	I LOVE LIFE	MANN	1993	NO	£15.00
N-100633	WASSERNAME!	TREMELOWE	1993	NO	£15.00
E-339134	SO YOU BOUGHT A COMPUTER?	HACKER	1994	ED	£10.99
E-339857	MATHS, GLORIOUS MATHS	ENTWHISTLE	1994	ED	£10.99
N-100997	COME IN NUMBER THREE	SPOONER	1993	NO	£15.00
N-100108	THE LAST LAUGH	MANN	1992	NO	£15.00
E-339687	USING YOUR COMPUTER	HACKER	1993	ED	£10.99
T-234397	UP THE CREEK!	HENDRIK	1994	TR	£12.50
T-234551	LIVING WITH CROCODILES	DEEPING	1992	TR	£12.50
E-339996	ENGLISH FOR EGGHEADS	CAWSON	1993	ED	£10.99
N-100304	THE WAY TO THE MOON	PERNELLE	1994	NO	£15.00
E-339400	EASY WAYS TO STUDY	ROUGHMAN	1993	ED	£10.99
N-100366	DEAD RINGER!	STOWELL	1994	NO	£15.00
N-100367	PIGEON PIE	SANSOME	1994	NO	£15.00
T-234900	DOWN AMONG THE DEADMEN	HENDRIK	1992	TR	£12.50
T-234588	LIVING WITH RHINOS	DEEPING	1993	TR	£12.50
T-234600	ELEPHANT INFANTS	DEEPING	1993	TR	£12.50
E-339807	LOGARITHMS MADE EASY	ENTWHISTLE	1992	ED	£10.99
E-339898	FRENCH FANTASIA	MARTINE	1994	ED	£10.99
N-100122	THE MASTER CALLS	SANSOME	1993	NO	£15.00
N-100555	FANCY THAT!	STOWELL	1993	NO	£15.00
T-234650	TIMBUCTOO OVERLAND	HENDRIK	1994	TR	£12.50
T-234700	ZULU COUNTRY	DEEPING	1992	TR	£12.50
E-339760	GENTLE GERMAN	WITZ	1994	ED	£10.99
E-339667	TEACH YOURSELF JAPANESE	YING	1993	ED	£10.99
E-339520	MULTIPLICATION MADNESS	ENTWHISTLE	1994	ED	£10.99

Question 4

REF NO	TITLE	AUTHOR	PUB.	CAT.	COST
N-100997	COME IN NUMBER THREE	SPOONER	1993	NO	£15.00
N-100366	DEAD RINGER!	STOWELL	1994	NO	£15.00
T-234900	DOWN AMONG THE DEADMEN	HENDRIK	1992	TR	£12.50
E-339400	EASY WAYS TO STUDY	ROUGHMAN	1993	ED	£10.99
T-234600	ELEPHANT INFANTS	DEEPING	1993	TR	£12.50
E-339996	ENGLISH FOR EGGHEADS	CAWSON	1993	ED	£10.99
N-100555	FANCY THAT!	STOWELL	1993	NO	£15.00
E-339898	FRENCH FANTASIA	MARTINE	1994	ED	£10.99
E-339760	GENTLE GERMAN	WITZ	1994	ED	£10.99
E-339211	HOW TO GET ON AT MATHS	ENTWHISTLE	1993	ED	£10.99
N-100662	I LOVE LIFE	MANN	1993	NO	£15.00
T-234551	LIVING WITH CROCODILES	DEEPING	1992	TR	£12.50
T-234588	LIVING WITH RHINOS	DEEPING	1993	TR	£12.50
E-339807	LOGARITHMS MADE EASY	ENTWHISTLE	1992	ED	£10.99
E-339857	MATHS, GLORIOUS MATHS	ENTWHISTLE	1994	ED	£10.99
E-339520	MULTIPLICATION MADNESS	ENTWHISTLE	1994	ED	£10.99
N-100367	PIGEON PIE	SANSOME	1994	NO	£15.00
E-339134	SO YOU BOUGHT A COMPUTER?	HACKER	1994	ED	£10.99
E-339667	TEACH YOURSELF JAPANESE	YING	1993	ED	£10.99
N-100108	THE LAST LAUGH	MANN	1992	NO	£15.00
N-100122	THE MASTER CALLS	SANSOME	1993	NO	£15.00
N-100304	THE WAY TO THE MOON	PERNELLE	1994	NO	£15.00
T-234339	THREE MILES DOWN	DEEPING	1994	TR	£12.50
T-234650	TIMBUCTOO OVERLAND	HENDRIK	1994	TR	£12.50
T-234760	TOO MANY COOKS	BAKE	1993	TR	£12.50
T-234397	UP THE CREEK!	HENDRIK	1994	TR	£12.50
E-339687	USING YOUR COMPUTER	HACKER	1993	ED	£10.99
N-100633	WASSERNAME!	TREMELOWE	1993	NO	£15.00
T-234700	ZULU COUNTRY	DEEPING	1992	TR	£12.50

Question 5

REF NO	TITLE	AUTHOR
E-339898	FRENCH FANTASIA	MARTINE
E-339760	GENTLE GERMAN	WITZ
E-339857	MATHS, GLORIOUS MATHS	ENTWHISTLE
E-339520	MULTIPLICATION MADNESS	ENTWHISTLE
E-339134	SO YOU BOUGHT A COMPUTER?	HACKER

Question 6

REF NO	TITLE	AUTHOR
T-234650	TIMBUCTOO OVERLAND	HENDRIK
T-234397	UP THE CREEK!	HENDRIK

Spreadsheet Solutions

Question 5

1994 PUBLICATIONS

Ref No	Author surname	No. of home sales	No. of export sales	Combined sales
T339	DEEPING	1565	65	1630
E134	HACKER	1980	69	2049
E857	ENTWHISTLE	2543	150	2693
T397	HENDRIK	2330	245	2575
N304	PERNELLE	7343	312	7655
N366	STOWELL	5650	1055	6705
N367	SANSOME	4340	1200	5540
E898	MARTINE	500	20	520
T650	HENDRIK	1986	406	2392
E760	WITZ	675	56	731
E520	ENTWHISTLE	1864	98	1962
TOTALS		30776	3676	34452

Question 7

1994 PUBLICATIONS

Ref No	Author surname	No. of home sales	No. of export sales	Combined sales	Cost per copy	Total income	Royalties 10%
T339	DEEPING	1565	65	1630	12.50	20375.00	2037.50
E134	HACKER	1980	69	2049	10.99	22518.51	2251.85
E857	ENTWHISTLE	2543	150	2693	10.99	29596.07	2959.61
T397	HENDRIK	2330	245	2575	12.50	32187.50	3218.75
N304	PERNELLE	7343	312	7655	15.00	114825.00	11482.50
N366	STOWELL	5650	1055	6705	15.00	100575.00	10057.50
N367	SANSOME	4340	1200	5540	15.00	83100.00	8310.00
E898	MARTINE	500	20	520	10.99	5714.80	571.48
T650	HENDRIK	1986	406	2392	12.50	29900.00	2990.00
E760	WITZ	675	56	731	10.99	8033.69	803.37
E520	ENTWHISTLE	1864	98	1962	10.99	21562.38	2156.24
TOTALS		30776	3676	34452		468387.95	46838.80

Question 7 - Formulae

1994 PUBLICATIONS

Ref No	Author surname	No. of home sales	No. of export sales	Combined sales	Cost per copy	Total income	Royalties 0.1
T339	DEEPING	1565	65	=D7+C7	12.5	=+E7*F7	=+G7*0.1
E134	HACKER	1980	69	=D8+C8	10.99	=+E8*F8	=+G8*0.1
E857	ENTWHISTLE	2543	150	=D9+C9	10.99	=+E9*F9	=+G9*0.1
T397	HENDRIK	2330	245	=D10+C10	12.5	=+E10*F10	=+G10*0.1
N304	PERNELLE	7343	312	=D11+C11	15	=+E11*F11	=+G11*0.1
N366	STOWELL	5650	1055	=D12+C12	15	=+E12*F12	=+G12*0.1
N367	SANSOME	4340	1200	=D13+C13	15	=+E13*F13	=+G13*0.1
E898	MARTINE	500	20	=D14+C14	10.99	=+E14*F14	=+G14*0.1
T650	HENDRIK	1986	406	=D15+C15	12.5	=+E15*F15	=+G15*0.1
E760	WITZ	675	56	=D16+C16	10.99	=+E16*F16	=+G16*0.1
E520	ENTWHISTLE	1864	98	=D17+C17	10.99	=+E17*F17	=+G17*0.1
TOTALS		=SUM(C7:C17)	=SUM(D7:D17)	=SUM(E7:E17)		=+SUM(G7:G17)	=+G20*0.1

Question 8

Ref No	No. of home sales	No. of export sales	Combined sales	Royalties 12%
TOTALS	30776	3676	34452	56206.55

Word Processing Solution

THE CITIZEN PUBLISHING COMPANY

Yearly Newsletter

As you know, we are committed to publishing quality books covering a variety of subjects and are proud to send you our latest fully illustrated, colour catalogue which we hope you will peruse with interest.

Our publishing house was founded in 1890 and we have now celebrated over one hundred years of service to the discerning reader. Our founder opened his first business in a small shed at the back of his own house using a hand-operated printing press. However, trade was so good, owing to the quality of his work, that he quickly outgrew those meagre premises, and the present purpose-built premises were erected on this site.

EXECUTIVE STAFF

General Manager	James MacKenzie	Ext 100
Chief Desk Editor	Alan Triscombe	Ext 201
Typesetter	Joe Mancewicz	Ext 350
Secretary	Helen Bryant	Ext 101

AUTHORS' ROYALTIES

At the beginning of this year we were worried that, owing to the general financial situation in the country as a whole, we may have had to reduce prices.

However, we are happy to say that we have been able to maintain the percentage paid to authors, and are even hoping to increase the amount paid, perhaps by 2%. Our Accountant is even now investigating the possibility, and the following figures illustrate the effect:

1

PUBLICATIONS

The majority of our publications can be classified into three main categories: Education, Travel and Novels, and the figure below illustrates graphically which sections of our publishing have been more successful than others. You will see that Novels are extrememly successful in the Home Sales market, while Education and Travel are 'struggling'.

What is immediately apparent from this graph and is a very worrying aspect, is the very low incidence of export sales in all categories. The Management has already launched a special investigation into the problem and the Committee is due to report in a few weeks.

AND NOW THE GOOD NEWS!

All is not doom and gloom, however, and although sales figures are not all we had hoped for, the number of educational books published during the year is very encouraging.

You will see that Brian Entwhistle continues to write for us, and his books are always popular in schools - especially with the introduction of 'GNVQ - A Mathematical Approach', and 'Maths is Fun', both books being scheduled for publication early next year.

We also have a number of new writers currently preparing text for other areas of GNVQ and shall be issuing further details in the near future.

2

Graphics Solution

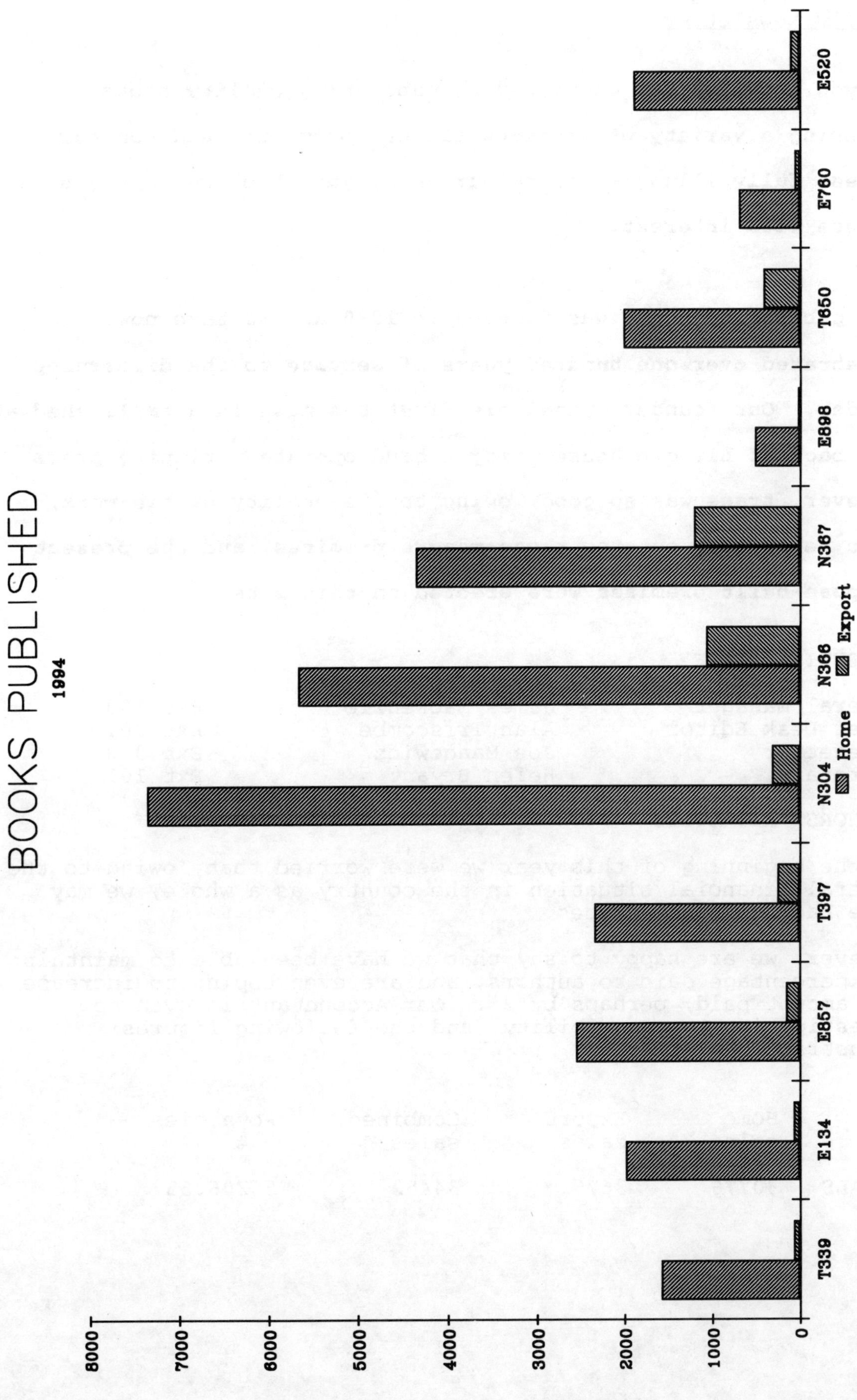

Collating Solution

THE CITIZEN PUBLISHING COMPANY

Yearly Newsletter

As you know, we are committed to publishing quality books covering a variety of subjects and are proud to send you our latest fully illustrated, colour catalogue which we hope you will peruse with interest.

Our publishing house was founded in 1890 and we have now celebrated over one hundred years of service to the discerning reader. Our founder opened his first business in a small shed at the back of his own house using a hand-operated printing press. However, trade was so good, owing to the quality of his work, that he quickly outgrew those meagre premises, and the present purpose-built premises were erected on this site.

EXECUTIVE STAFF

General Manager	James MacKenzie	Ext 100
Chief Desk Editor	Alan Triscombe	Ext 201
Typesetter	Joe Mancewicz	Ext 350
Secretary	Helen Bryant	Ext 101

AUTHORS' ROYALTIES

At the beginning of this year we were worried that, owing to the general financial situation in the country as a whole, we may have had to reduce prices.

However, we are happy to say that we have been able to maintain the percentage paid to authors, and are even hoping to increase the amount paid, perhaps by 2%. Our Accountant is even now investigating the possibility, and the following figures illustrate the effect:

	Home sales	Export sales	Combined sales	Royalties 12%
TOTALS	30776	3676	34452	56206.55

1

PUBLICATIONS

The majority of our publications can be classified into three main categories: Education, Travel and Novels, and the figure below illustrates graphically which sections of our publishing have been more successful than others. You will see that Novels are extrememly successful in the Home Sales market, while Education and Travel are 'struggling'.

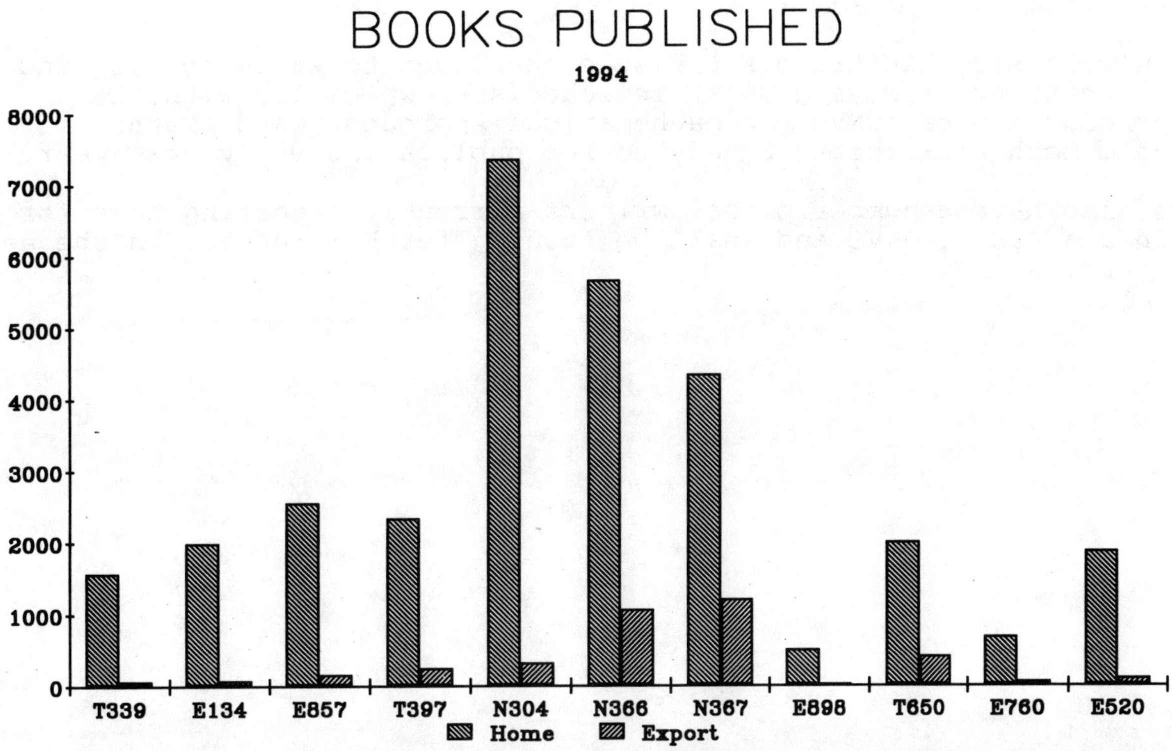

What is immediately apparent from this graph and is a very worrying aspect, is the very low incidence of export sales in all categories. The Management has already launched a special investigation into the problem and the Committee is due to report in a few weeks.

2

AND NOW THE GOOD NEWS!

All is not doom and gloom, however, and although sales figures are not all we had hoped for, the number of educational books published during the year is very encouraging.

REF NO	TITLE	AUTHOR SURNAME
E-339898	FRENCH FANTASIA	MARTINE
E-339760	GENTLE GERMAN	WITZ
E-339857	MATHS, GLORIOUS MATHS	ENTWHISTLE
E-339520	MULTIPLICATION MADNESS	ENTWHISTLE
E-339134	SO YOU BOUGHT A COMPUTER?	HACKER

You will see that Brian Entwhistle continues to write for us, and his books are always popular in schools - especially with the introduction of 'GNVQ - A Mathematical Approach', and 'Maths is Fun', both books being scheduled for publication early next year.

We also have a number of new writers currently preparing text for other areas of GNVQ and shall be issuing further details in the near future.

3

Horticultural Show

Database Solutions

Question 3a
(The database contains 31 records)

NAME	COLOUR	HEIGHT	POSITION	TYPE
ACHILLEA	YELLOW	150	M	P
ALSTROMERIA	PINK	75	M	P
ANTIRRHINUM	MIXED	45	WS	HHA
ASTILBE	CREAM	200	M	P
CAMPANULA	BLUE	20	WS	HHA
CATMINT	BLUE	40	M	P
CINERARIA	SILVER	20	WS	HHA
COSMOS	PINK	100	S	HHA
CYCLAMEN	PINK	15	SH	P
DELPHINIUM	BLUE	130	S	HA
DIANTHUS	WHITE	20	WS	HHA
DIMORPHOTHECA	YELLOW	30	S	HA
DOG ROSE	PINK	300	M	WD
ECHINOPS	BLUE	100	S	P
FOXGLOVE	PINK	100	SH	WD
GYPSOPHILA	WHITE	36	S	HA
HELICHRYSUM	MIXED	45	S	HA
HOSTA	GREEN	60	SH	P
LUPIN	MIXED	30	S	HA
MECONOPSIS	BLUE	90	SH	P
MIMULUS	ORANGE	28	M	HHA
PANSY	MIXED	15	M	P
PETUNIA	RED	30	M	HHA
PRIMROSE	YELLOW	15	S	WD
SEMPERFLORENS	MIXED	15	WS	HHA
SOLIDAGO	YELLOW	60	M	P
STOCK	PINK	70	S	HHA
SUNFLOWER	YELLOW	200	S	HA
TOADFLAX	YELLOW	60	S	WD
TROLLIUS	YELLOW	40	SH	P
VERBENA	RED	30	S	HHA

Question 3b

NAME	COLOUR	HEIGHT	POSITION	TYPE
ACHILLEA	YELLOW	150	M	P
SOLIDAGO	YELLOW	60	M	P

Question 3c

HEIGHT	NAME
20	CAMPANULA
20	CINERARIA
15	CYCLAMEN
20	DIANTHUS
15	PANSY
15	PRIMROSE
15	SEMPERFLORENS

Question 3d

NAME	COLOUR	HEIGHT	POSITION	TYPE
ACHILLEA	YELLOW	150	M	P
DIMORPHOTHECA	YELLOW	30	S	HA
PRIMROSE	YELLOW	15	S	WD
SOLIDAGO	YELLOW	60	M	P
SUNFLOWER	YELLOW	200	S	HA
TOADFLAX	YELLOW	60	S	WD
TROLLIUS	YELLOW	40	SH	P

Question 3e

NAME	POSITION
ANTIRRHINUM	WS
HELICHRYSUM	S
LUPIN	S
PANSY	M
SEMPERFLORENS	WS

Question 3f

NAME	COLOUR	HEIGHT
CYCLAMEN	PINK	15
FOXGLOVE	PINK	100
HOSTA	GREEN	60
MECONOPSIS	BLUE	90
TROLLIUS	YELLOW	40

Question 3g

NAME	COLOUR
ANTIRRHINUM	MIXED
CAMPANULA	BLUE
CINERARIA	SILVER
DIANTHUS	WHITE
SEMPERFLORENS	MIXED

Spreadsheet Solutions

Question 3

County Horticultural Show

Income

	Year 1	Year 2	Year 3	Year 4	Year 5
Entry fees					
Vegetables	0.50	0.60	0.70	0.90	1.10
Flowers	0.40	0.50	0.60	0.80	1.00
Handicrafts	0.30	0.40	0.50	0.70	0.90
No. of entrants					
Vegetables	120	125	156	160	160
Flowers	200	220	255	280	300
Handicrafts	90	100	120	125	150
Total entry fees					
Veg	60.00	75.00	109.20	144.00	176.00
Flowers	80.00	110.00	153.00	224.00	300.00
Handicrafts	27.00	40.00	60.00	87.50	135.00
Sales	200.00	210.00	220.50	231.53	243.10
Total income	367.00	435.00	542.70	687.03	854.10
Expenditure					
Printing	150.00	150.00	150.00	150.00	150.00
Hire	250.00	250.00	250.00	250.00	250.00
Fees	80.00	82.00	84.05	86.15	88.31
Total expenditure	480.00	482.00	484.05	486.15	488.31
Profit/Loss	-113.00	-47.00	58.65	200.88	365.79

Question 4

County Horticultural Show

Income

	Year 1	Year 2	Year 3	Year 4	Year 5
Entry fees					
Vegetables	0.5	0.6	0.7	0.9	1.1
Flowers	0.4	0.5	0.6	0.8	1
Handicrafts	0.3	0.4	0.5	0.7	0.9
No. of entrants					
Vegetables	120	125	156	160	160
Flowers	200	220	255	280	300
Handicrafts	90	100	120	125	150
Total entry fees					
Veg	60	75	109.2	144	176
Flowers	80	110	153	224	300
Handicrafts	27	40	60	87.5	135
Sales	200	210	220.5	231.53	243.1
Total income	=SUM(B25:B29)	=SUM(C25:C29)	=SUM(D25:D29)	=SUM(E25:E29)	=SUM(F25:F29)
Expenditure					
Printing	150	150	150	150	150
Hire	250	250	250	250	250
Fees	80	=+B37+B37*0.025	=+C37+C37*0.025	=+D37+D37*0.025	=+E37+E37*0.025
Total expenditure	=SUM(B35:B37)	=SUM(C35:C37)	=SUM(D35:D37)	=SUM(E35:E37)	=SUM(F35:F37)
Profit/Loss	=+B31-B40	=+C31-C40	=+D31-D40	=+E31-E40	=+F31-F40

Question 6

County Horticultural Show

Income

	Year 1	Year 2	Year 3	Year 4	Year 5	Year 6
Entry fees						
Vegetables	0.50	0.60	0.70	0.90	1.10	1.10
Flowers	0.40	0.50	0.60	0.80	1.00	1.00
Handicrafts	0.30	0.40	0.50	0.70	0.90	0.90
No. of entrants						
Vegetables	120	125	156	160	160	160
Flowers	200	220	255	280	300	300
Handicrafts	90	100	120	125	150	150
Total entry fees						
Veg	60.00	75.00	109.20	144.00	176.00	176.00
Flowers	80.00	110.00	153.00	224.00	300.00	300.00
Handicrafts	27.00	40.00	60.00	87.50	135.00	135.00
Sales	200.00	210.00	220.50	231.53	243.10	255.26
Total income	367.00	435.00	542.70	687.03	854.10	866.26
Expenditure						
Printing	150.00	150.00	150.00	150.00	150.00	150.00
Hire	250.00	250.00	250.00	250.00	250.00	356.00
Fees	80.00	82.00	84.05	86.15	88.31	88.31
Total expenditure	480.00	482.00	484.05	486.15	488.31	594.31
Profit/Loss	-113.00	-47.00	58.65	200.88	365.79	271.95

Word Processing Solution

COUNTY HORTICULTURAL SHOW

COMMITTEE MEMBERS

Chairperson	J AMOS	336529
Secretary	B SMITH	22198
Treasurer	F SHAW	66583
Schedules	H FORD	98611
Entertainment	V JAMES	66928

We are proud to present our schedule for the forthcoming horticultural show, and we think you will agree that it is the most exciting in the history of the Show. We have retained all the old familiar classes which have proved to be popular with you all over the past years; but we have included several new (and perhaps a little unusual) classes, which have been suggested to us by entrants - these are numbered 104-109 in the schedule and we hope you will find them interesting and challenging. Please let the Committee know your thoughts on these innovations and also let us know if you have any constructive suggestions or new ideas.

ENTRIES

Entries in all classes have been rising steadily since our first year and we are particularly pleased with the increase in the Handicraft entries, as these started off so hesitantly in the first year.

1

ENTRY FEES

The Committee has decided that because the entry fees have risen steadily over the last few years, it is advisable to retain the present level, and not increase them again. A recommendation is to be put to the next AGM to the effect that fees should be "frozen" at the present level, at least for the next two years.

ENTERTAINMENT

The organisation for this year's show is progressing satisfactorily, and the Secretary has already booked several people who are coming to display their crafts. Amongst these is the local potter, Michelle Destang, whose work has been chosen for display by a very famous London store; and Terry Michell with his beautiful long case clocks, all lovingly made by hand.

We also hope to have a dancing display by the "Irish Shamrocks", the newly formed dancing troupe, as well as a demonstration of dog handling by the Police Dog Association and pony rides for the children. Altogether, we are sure you will agree, a good mixture for a successful day.

COMPETITION

Another innovation that we are introducing this year is a competition specially for children. We have produced free packets of the following seeds which are available to any child who would like to contact the Secretary. One of the new classes will be for the best flowers produced from the seeds. A list of the seeds available is given below for your information.

LAYOUT OF SITE

We are very fortunate this year in having obtained the services of Lt Col Brian Chichester, who is organising the layout of the site. Those of you who attended the show last year will remember that one or two of the outside exhibitors' stands were not very accessible, and Brian is drawing up a plan which will ensure that every stallholder will have a prime position. He will also include in his design a suitable open space for the demonstrations and the dancing display. We look forward to seeing the outcome of all his hard work.

2

Graphics Solution

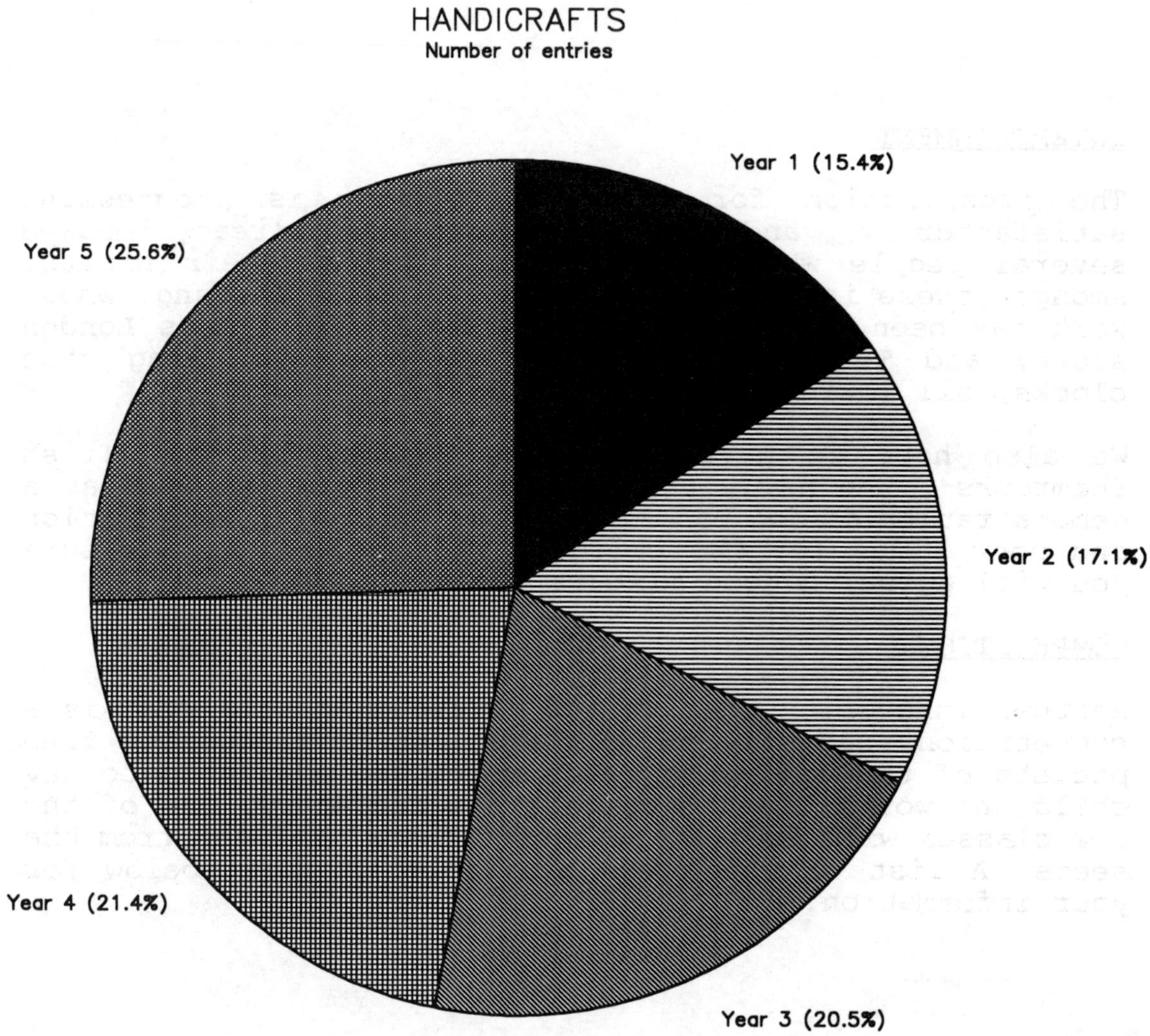

Collating Solution

COUNTY HORTICULTURAL SHOW

COMMITTEE MEMBERS

Chairperson	J AMOS	336529
Secretary	B SMITH	22198
Treasurer	F SHAW	66583
Schedules	H FORD	98611
Entertainment	V JAMES	66928

We are proud to present our schedule for the forthcoming horticultural show, and we think you will agree that it is the most exciting in the history of the Show. We have retained all the old familiar classes which have proved to be popular with you all over the past years; but we have included several new (and perhaps a little unusual) classes, which have been suggested to us by entrants - these are numbered 104-109 in the schedule and we hope you will find them interesting and challenging. Please let the Committee know your thoughts on these innovations and also let us know if you have any constructive suggestions or new ideas.

ENTRIES

Entries in all classes have been rising steadily since our first year and we are particularly pleased with the increase in the Handicraft entries, as these started off so hesitantly in the first year.

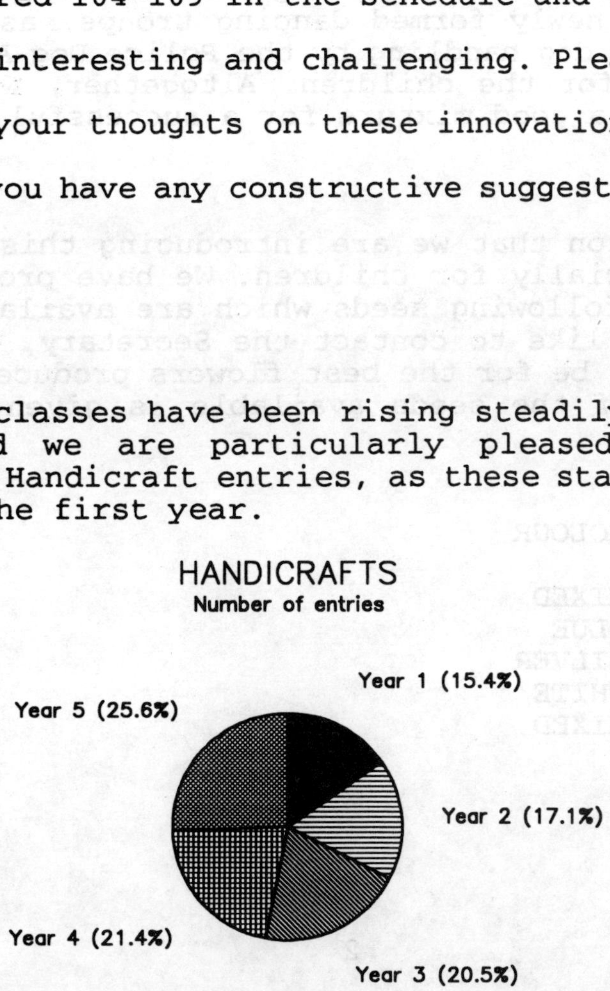

1

ENTRY FEES

The Committee has decided that because the entry fees have risen steadily over the last few years, it is advisable to retain the present level, and not increase them again. A recommendation is to be put to the next AGM to the effect that fees should be "frozen" at the present level, at least for the next two years.

	Year 1	Year 2	Year 3	Year 4	Year 5
Veg	0.50	0.60	0.70	0.90	1.10
Flowers	0.40	0.50	0.60	0.80	1.00
Handicrafts	0.30	0.40	0.50	0.70	0.90

ENTERTAINMENT

The organisation for this year's show is progressing satisfactorily, and the Secretary has already booked several people who are coming to display their crafts. Amongst these is the local potter, Michelle Destang, whose work has been chosen for display by a very famous London store; and Terry Michell with his beautiful long case clocks, all lovingly made by hand.

We also hope to have a dancing display by the "Irish Shamrocks", the newly formed dancing troupe, as well as a demonstration of dog handling by the Police Dog Association and pony rides for the children. Altogether, we are sure you will agree, a good mixture for a successful day.

COMPETITION

Another innovation that we are introducing this year is a competition specially for children. We have produced free packets of the following seeds which are available to any child who would like to contact the Secretary. One of the new classes will be for the best flowers produced from the seeds. A list of the seeds available is given below for your information.

NAME	COLOUR
ANTIRRHINUM	MIXED
CAMPANULA	BLUE
CINERARIA	SILVER
DIANTHUS	WHITE
SEMERFLORENS	MIXED

2

LAYOUT OF SITE

We are very fortunate this year in having obtained the services of Lt Col Brian Chichester, who is organising the layout of the site. Those of you who attended the show last year will remember that one or two of the outside exhibitors' stands were not very accessible, and Brian is drawing up a plan which will ensure that every stallholder will have a prime position. He will also include in his design a suitable open space for the demonstrations and the dancing display. We look forward to seeing the outcome of all his hard work.

3

College Courses

Database Solutions

Question 2a
(The database consists of 33 records)

SURNAME	FORENAME	SEX	DoB	APP	SUGG	GCSE	O	A
ABBOTT	LOUISA	F	07.12.79	N	R	3		
ANDREWS	BRIAN	M	10.10.78	R	R	4	1	
BAKER	CYNTHIA	F	09.06.78	S	S	6		
BELTON	FRANCES	F	07.07.77	S	S		6	1
BICKER	WILLIAM	M	10.10.79	R	R	1		
BLESSED	BRIAN	M	08.08.77	R	N	3	2	
BRINDLEY	CHRISTOPHER	M	05.09.77	N	N		5	
CHILDS	CHRISTINE	F	24.07.79	N	N		3	
CLARKE	LISA	F	15.05.78	R	S		6	2
COCHRANE	ANTHEA	F	07.08.78	S	S	5		1
DAVIS	DAVID	M	13.09.78	N	S			4
FINN	IRENE	F	03.09.79	N	R	1		
FOTHERINGHAM	TOM	M	17.11.77	N	R	2		
FRANCIS	MARY	F	22.02.78	N	N	3		
FREEMAN	RACHEL	F	04.03.79	N	S	3		
GIBSON	STELLA	F	02.05.79	R	R	1		
GRAHAM	STAN	M	05.02.78	N	N	1	3	
GRANT	JACKIE	F	12.12.79	N	R			
HARDING	JEAN	F	06.01.77	S	S	5	1	
JENKINS	MAUREEN	F	05.06.78	S	S		10	3
KITCHENER	SIMONE	F	05.06.77	S	S		5	1
LIPTON	MAY	F	15.06.78	N	N		1	
LYON	DEBBIE	F	03.06.77	S	S		5	
MCNAUGHT	COLIN	M	14.07.79	R	R			
REDSTON	KEITH	M	21.05.79	N	N	1		
ROBERTS	KELLY	F	15.01.79	S	R	1		
RUCK	MAUREEN	F	25.12.76	R	R	2		
RULE	JENNIFER	F	01.01.78	N	N		1	
SCAMELL	KAREN	F	15.03.78	N	S		4	2
SMITHERS	JOANNE	F	10.09.79	S	N	3		
THOMPSON	HEATHER	F	16.02.79	N	N	3		
TRUCKLE	ROSEMARIE	F	01.01.79	N	N	3		
WINGFIELD	IVY	F	15.07.79	R	R	1		

Question 2b

SURNAME	FORENAME	DoB	APP	SUGG
BAKER	CYNTHIA	09.06.78	S	S
BELTON	FRANCES	07.07.77	S	S
COCHRANE	ANTHEA	07.08.78	S	S
HARDING	JEAN	06.01.77	S	S
JENKINS	MAUREEN	05.06.78	S	S
KITCHENER	SIMONE	05.06.77	S	S
LYON	DEBBIE	03.06.77	S	S

Question 2c

SURNAME	FORENAME	GCSE	O	A
BRINDLEY	CHRISTOPHER		5	
CHILDS	CHRISTINE		3	
GRAHAM	STAN	1	3	
LIPTON	MAY		1	
RULE	JENNIFER		1	

Question 2d

SURNAME	FORENAME	DoB
WINGFIELD	IVY	15.07.79
TRUCKLE	ROSEMARIE	01.01.79
THOMPSON	HEATHER	16.02.79
SMITHERS	JOANNE	10.09.79
SCAMELL	KAREN	15.03.78
RULE	JENNIFER	01.01.78
RUCK	MAUREEN	25.12.76
ROBERTS	KELLY	15.01.79
REDSTON	KEITH	21.05.79
MCNAUGHT	COLIN	14.07.79
LYON	DEBBIE	03.06.77
LIPTON	MAY	15.06.78
KITCHENER	SIMONE	05.06.77
JENKINS	MAUREEN	05.06.78
HARDING	JEAN	06.01.77
GRANT	JACKIE	12.12.79
GRAHAM	STAN	05.02.78
GIBSON	STELLA	02.05.79
FREEMAN	RACHEL	04.03.79
FRANCIS	MARY	22.02.78
FOTHERINGHAM	TOM	17.11.77
FINN	IRENE	03.09.79
DAVIS	DAVID	13.09.78
COCHRANE	ANTHEA	07.08.78
CLARKE	LISA	15.05.78
CHILDS	CHRISTINE	24.07.79
BRINDLEY	CHRISTOPHER	05.09.77
BLESSED	BRIAN	08.08.77
BICKER	WILLIAM	10.10.79
BELTON	FRANCES	07.07.77
BAKER	CYNTHIA	09.06.78
ANDREWS	BRIAN	10.10.78
ABBOTT	LOUISA	07.12.79

Question 2e

SURNAME	SEX	SUGG	GCSE
ANDREWS	M	R	4
ABBOTT	F	R	3

Spreadsheet Solutions

Question 3

Leisure Courses

Income

	No. of classes	No. of students	Class fee	Total fees
Batik	20	10	3.50	700.00
Wood Turning	20	10	3.50	700.00
Fly Fishing	20	10	5.00	1000.00
Upholstery	36	15	3.50	1890.00
Calligraphy	36	15	4.50	2430.00
Cake Decorating	36	15	8.00	4320.00
Totals	168			11040.00

Books and stationery

	No. of students	Cost	
	75	18.00	1350.00
Total			12390.00

Outgoings per class	Cost	No. of classes	
Salaries	12.50	168	2100.00
Hire of Bldg	25.00	168	4200.00
Heat/Light	15.00	168	2520.00
Caretaker's Sal	10.50	168	1764.00
Total			10584.00
Profit			1806.00

Question 4 - Formulae

Leisure Courses

Income

	No. of classes	No. of students	Class fee	Total fees
Batik	20	10	3.5	=B8*C8*D8
Wood Turning	20	10	3.5	=B9*C9*D9
Fly Fishing	20	10	5	=B10*C10*D10
Upholstery	36	15	3.5	=B11*C11*D11
Calligraphy	36	15	4.5	=B12*C12*D12
Cake Decorating	36	15	8	=B13*C13*D13
Totals	=+SUM(B8:B13)			=+SUM(E8:E13)

Books and stationery

		No. of students	Cost	
		=SUM(C8:C14)	18	=C23*D23
Total				=+E23+E15

Outgoings per class	Cost	No. of classes		
Salaries	12.5	168		=B34*C34
Hire of Bldg	25	168		=B35*C35
Heat/Light	15	168		=B36*C36
Caretaker's Salary	10.5	168		=B37*C37
Total				=SUM(E34:E37)
Profit				=SUM(E27-E39)

Question 5

Outgoings per class	Cost	No. of classes	
Salaries	13.50	168	2268.00
Hire of Bldg	25.00	168	4200.00
Heat/Light	15.00	168	2520.00
Caretaker's Sal	10.50	168	1764.00
Total			10752.00

Question 6

Income

	No. of classes	Total fees
Batik	20	700.00
Wood Turning	20	700.00
Fly Fishing	20	1000.00
Upholstery	36	1890.00
Calligraphy	36	2430.00
Cake Decorating	36	4320.00
Photography	9	1620.00
Totals	177	12660.00

Word Processing Solution

DEPARTMENT OF BUSINESS AND TECHNOLOGY

The Department provides a variety of full-time courses for those students who intend to pursue a career in Business Management or Office Administration in either the public or private sectors of industry and commerce. The business world is one that is both exciting and rapidly changing, and so the range and content of our courses is always being updated to meet the new demands of employers and students.

R A N G E   O F   C O U R S E S

The following gives the complete range of courses that we shall be offering this year:

Modern Languages	Secretarial
National Vocational Qualification	Office Skills
Private Secretary's Certificate	Hotel Reception

L A N G U A G E S

Particular attention is drawn to the Modern Languages Course which is designed for post 'A' level students who wish to apply their language skills in a secretarial or business context.

The Department is in the process of acquiring a new integrated micro-electronic language laboratory to add to its already extensive range of audio-visual equipment.

S E C R E T A R I A L

The Department has for some time offered a full-time, one-year course leading to the <u>LCCI Private Secretary's Certificate</u>. This is a prestigious course and we can only accept limited numbers - the following having been chosen so far from a short list of 30.

S T A T E   O F   T H E   A R T   E Q U I P M E N T

The facilities of the Department reflect the increasing influence of new technology in the office, and its importance in further and higher education courses. The typewriting rooms are fitted with the latest electronic

1

typewriters and audio equipment. The Training Office and Office Practice Workshop have been designed to reflect modern business methods, and utilise the new technology, and are equipped with off-set litho, fax, colour photocopying, etc.

C O M P U T I N G

There are now four micro-computing rooms with modern hardware and a variety of software for data processing and word processing, as well as for use in other business studies subjects, eg Accounting and Economics, and for practical business simulations.

C O U R S E   A P P L I C A T I O N S

We are pleased to see that applications for next year's courses are coming in at a steady pace, and at the time of writing the position is as follows:

T H E   A N N E X E   H I R I N G

Since we moved into our new premises the old annexe has been unused, but this year our own Community Arts Section is proposing to hire the building for some of their leisure classes, and to put the whole scheme on a commercial footing. Mr Bottomley has prepared some figures giving the estimated income for the year.

Perhaps we should start charging for all our classes - it certainly seems very profitable!

2

Graphics Solution

Collating Solution

DEPARTMENT OF BUSINESS AND TECHNOLOGY

The Department provides a variety of full-time courses for those students who intend to pursue a career in Business Management or Office Administration in either the public or private sectors of industry and commerce. The business world is one that is both exciting and rapidly changing, and so the range and content of our courses is always being updated to meet the new demands of employers and students.

R A N G E   O F   C O U R S E S

The following gives the complete range of courses that we shall be offering this year:

Modern Languages	Secretarial
National Vocational Qualification	Office Skills
Private Secretary's Certificate	Hotel Reception

L A N G U A G E S

Particular attention is drawn to the Modern Languages Course which is designed for post "A" level students who wish to apply their language skills in a secretarial or business context.

The Department is in the process of acquiring a new integrated micro-electronic language laboratory to add to its already extensive range of audio-visual equipment.

S E C R E T A R I A L

The Department has for some time offered a full-time, one-year course leading to the LCCI Private Secretary's Certificate. This is a prestigious course and we can only accept limited numbers - the following having been chosen so far from a short list of 30.

SURNAME	FORENAME	DoB	APP	SUGG
BAKER	CYNTHIA	09.06.78	S	S
BELTON	FRANCES	07.07.77	S	S
COCHRANE	ANTHEA	07.08.78	S	S
HARDING	JEAN	06.01.77	S	S
JENKINS	MAUREEN	05.06.78	S	S
KITCHENER	SIMONE	05.06.77	S	S
LYON	DEBBIE	03.06.77	S	S

1

S T A T E   O F   T H E   A R T   E Q U I P M E N T

The facilities of the Department reflect the increasing influence of new technology in the office, and its importance in further and higher education courses. The typewriting rooms are fitted with the latest electronic typewriters and audio equipment. The Training Office and Office Practice Workshop have been designed to reflect modern business methods, and utilise the new technology, and are equipped with off-set litho, fax, colour photocopying, etc.

C O M P U T I N G

There are now four micro-computing rooms with modern hardware and a variety of software for data processing and word processing, as well as for use in other business studies subjects, eg Accounting and Economics, and for practical business simulations.

C O U R S E   A P P L I C A T I O N S

We are pleased to see that applications for next year's courses are coming in at a steady pace, and at the time of writing the position is as follows:

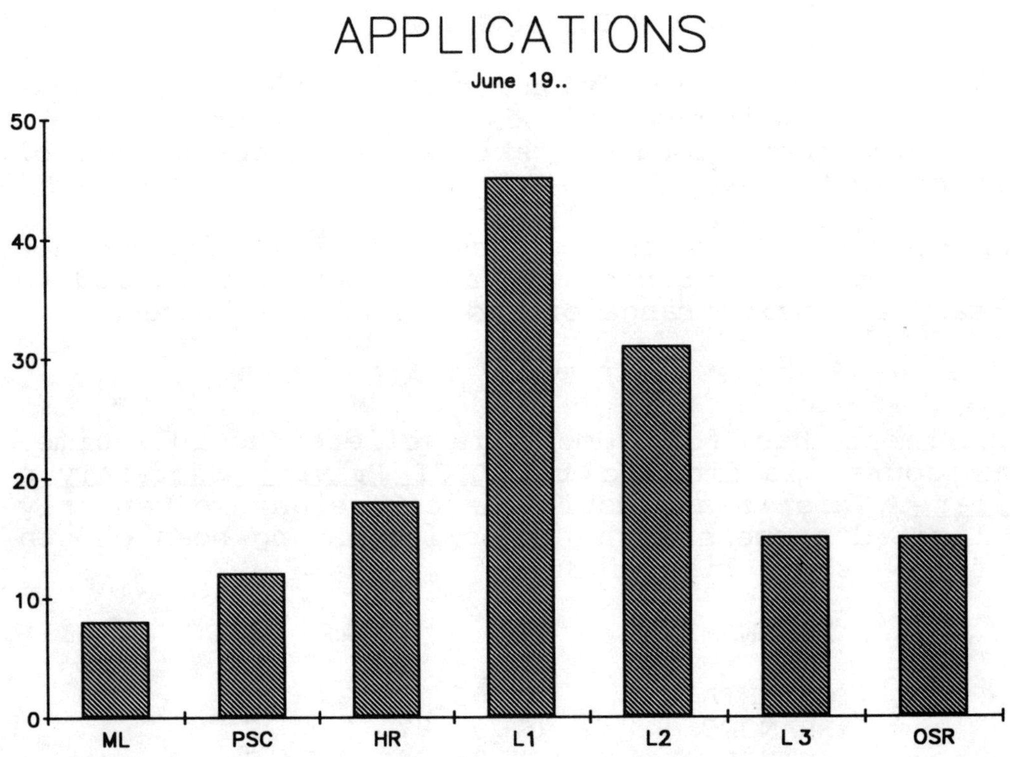

2

THE ANNEXE HIRING

Since we moved into our new premises the old annexe has been unused, but this year our own Community Arts Section is proposing to hire the building for some of their leisure classes, and to put the whole scheme on a commercial footing. Mr Bottomley has prepared some figures giving the estimated income for the year.

INCOME

	No. of classes	No. of students	Class fee	Total fees
Batik	20	10	3.50	700.00
Wood Turning	20	10	3.50	700.00
Fly Fishing	20	10	5.00	1000.00
Upholstery	36	15	3.50	1890.00
Calligraphy	36	15	4.50	2430.00
Cake Decorating	36	15	8.00	4320.00
Photography	9	12	15.00	1620.00
Totals	177			12660.00

Books and stationery	No. of students	Cost	
	87	18.00	1566.00

Perhaps we should start charging for all our classes - it certainly seems very profitable!

3

Hotel Accommodation

Database Solutions

Question 3a
(The database consists of 30 records)

HOTEL NAME	TOWN	TEL NO	MANAGER	WE	CO	PP	FVM	DIST
ABBEY HOUSE	ST BERNARD'S	29718	MEADER C	YES	NO	YES	YES	11
AMBLESIDE	MAPLEDENE	43106	GREENE K	YES	NO	YES	N	20
ATHENE	BROUGHTON ABBEY	660044	SUTTON B R	YES	NO	YES	YES	5
BISHOP'S LODGE	ST BERNARD'S	66723	LOVELL B	YES	YES	YES	NO	11
BRITANNIA	LOWER CHERRINGTON	467	CHESTERTON J	YES	NO	NO	NO	3
BRYANSCOMBE	FORDTOWN	66328	CANNING R	NO	YES	YES	NO	7
BURNHAM GRANGE	BURNHAM	36911	MUGOMBA A	YES	YES	YES	YES	12
CANTALOUPE	FORDTOWN	116387	FORDHAM G	YES	YES	NO	NO	7
COLEBROOK	ILCHESTER	32107	NORTON M	YES	NO	YES	YES	8
COLLEGE COURT	LORDCOMBE	323711	BRAIN G	YES	NO	YES	NO	9
COMBE HOTEL	LORDCOMBE	89119	LORD P	YES	YES	YES	NO	9
COPPLESTONE HOUSE	COPPLESTONE	23610	TORRES H	YES	YES	YES	NO	10
CORDON HOUSE	INCHESTER	29818	GORDON S	YES	NO	YES	NO	8
COUNTRY HOUSE	MAPLEDENE	22583	CORY N	YES	NO	YES	NO	20
COUNTY	BURNHAM	113291	CROUCH J	YES	YES	YES	YES	12
FORDTON MANOR	FORDTON	16355	KNIGHT T	YES	NO	YES	NO	7
IVANHOE	LORDCOMBE	89118	DAVIES M	NO	YES	YES	YES	9
LORDCOMBE MANOR	LORDCOMBE	44587	ADAMS J	YES	YES	YES	YES	9
MAPLES	FORDTOWN	660043	SMITH B	YES	NO	YES	NO	7
MILLSTREAM HOTEL	COPPLESTONE	22236	SEDDON J	YES	YES	NO	YES	10
MOAT HOUSE	COPPLESTONE	33771	MAYNARD B	YES	NO	YES	NO	10
RESTAWHILE	FORDTOWN	29973	GRINTER J	YES	YES	YES	YES	7
ROBBINS	BURNHAM	21007	BYRD R	NO	YES	YES	YES	12
ST BERNARD'S ABBEY	ST BERNARD'S	22919	MONK B	NO	YES	YES	YES	11
THE ACROPOLIS	EXETER	410633	ROLFS P	YES	YES	YES	YES	10
THE BRINSMEAD	EXETER	41077	WATERHOUSE K	YES	YES	YES	NO	7
THE ROYAL CAVALIER	STEEPLE UNDER WYCHWOOD	667353	BARCLAY B J	YES	YES	NO	NO	8
THROOPE HOUSE	BURNHAM	61809	BROOKE R	YES	NO	YES	YES	12
TRELAWNY HOTEL	INCHESTER	34690	COOKE J	YES	NO	YES	NO	8
WHITE HART	MAPLEDENE	99160	FORTESCUE D	YES	NO	YES	YES	20

Question 3b

HOTEL NAME	TOWN	TEL NO	MANAGER	WE	CO	PP	FVM	DIST
THE BRINSMEAD	EXETER	41077	WATERHOUSE K	YES	YES	YES	NO	7
COPPLESTONE HOUSE	COPPLESTONE	23610	TORRES H	YES	YES	YES	NO	10
ATHENE	BROUGHTON ABBEY	660044	SUTTON B R	YES	NO	YES	YES	5
MAPLES	FORDTOWN	660043	SMITH B	YES	NO	YES	NO	7
MILLSTREAM HOTEL	COPPLESTONE	22236	SEDDON J	YES	YES	NO	YES	10
THE ACROPOLIS	EXETER	410633	ROLFS P	YES	YES	YES	YES	10
COLEBROOK	ILCHESTER	32107	NORTON M	YES	NO	YES	YES	8
BURNHAM GRANGE	BURNHAM	36911	MUGOMBA A	YES	YES	YES	YES	12
ST BERNARD'S ABBEY	ST BERNARD'S	22919	MONK B	NO	YES	YES	YES	11
ABBEY HOUSE	ST BERNARD'S	29718	MEADER C	YES	NO	YES	YES	11
MOAT HOUSE	COPPLESTONE	33771	MAYNARD B	YES	NO	YES	NO	10
BISHOP'S LODGE	ST BERNARD'S	66723	LOVELL B	YES	YES	YES	NO	11
COMBE HOTEL	LORDCOMBE	89119	LORD P	YES	YES	YES	NO	9
FORDTON MANOR	FORDTON	16355	KNIGHT T	YES	NO	YES	NO	7
RESTAWHILE	FORDTOWN	29973	GRINTER J	YES	YES	YES	YES	7
AMBLESIDE	MAPLEDENE	43106	GREENE K	YES	NO	YES	N	20
CORDON HOUSE	INCHESTER	29818	GORDON S	YES	NO	YES	NO	8
WHITE HART	MAPLEDENE	99160	FORTESCUE D	YES	NO	YES	YES	20
CANTALOUPE	FORDTOWN	116387	FORDHAM G	YES	YES	NO	NO	7
IVANHOE	LORDCOMBE	89118	DAVIES M	NO	YES	YES	YES	9
COUNTY	BURNHAM	113291	CROUCH J	YES	YES	YES	YES	12
COUNTRY HOUSE	MAPLEDENE	22583	CORY N	YES	NO	YES	NO	20
TRELAWNY HOTEL	INCHESTER	34690	COOKE J	YES	NO	YES	NO	8
BRITANNIA	LOWER CHERRINGTON	467	CHESTERTON J	YES	NO	NO	NO	3
BRYANSCOMBE	FORDTOWN	66328	CANNING R	NO	YES	YES	NO	7
ROBBINS	BURNHAM	21007	BYRD R	NO	YES	YES	YES	12
THROOPE HOUSE	BURNHAM	61809	BROOKE R	YES	NO	YES	YES	12
COLLEGE COURT	LORDCOMBE	323711	BRAIN G	YES	NO	YES	NO	9
THE ROYAL CAVALIER	STEEPLE UNDER WYCHWOOD	667353	BARCLAY B J	YES	YES	NO	NO	8
LORDCOMBE MANOR	LORDCOMBE	44587	ADAMS J	YES	YES	YES	YES	9

Question 3c

HOTEL NAME	TOWN	TEL NO
BURNHAM GRANGE	BURNHAM	36911
COUNTY	BURNHAM	113291
ROBBINS	BURNHAM	21007
THROOPE HOUSE	BURNHAM	61809

Question 3d

HOTEL NAME	TEL NO	MANAGER
THE BRINSMEAD	41077	WATERHOUSE K
ATHENE	660044	SUTTON B R
MAPLES	660043	SMITH B
FORDTON MANOR	16355	KNIGHT T
RESTAWHILE	29973	GRINTER J

Question 3e

HOTEL NAME
THE BRINSMEAD
COPPLESTONE HOUSE
MILLSTREAM HOTEL
THE ACROPOLIS
BURNHAM GRANGE
ST BERNARD'S ABBEY
BISHOP'S LODGE
COMBE HOTEL
RESTAWHILE
CANTALOUPE
IVANHOE
COUNTY
BRYANSCOMBE
ROBBINS
THE ROYAL CAVALIER
LORDCOMBE MANOR

Spreadsheet Solutions

Question 2

Comparative Costs for Wedding (60 guests)

	Cavalier	Britannia	Athene
HALL	500.00	320.00	300.00
CAKE	250.00	150.00	200.00
MC	50.00	0.00	50.00
REST ROOM	60.00	10.50	0.00
PHOTOGRAPHER	100.00	125.00	180.00
TOTAL	960.00	605.50	730.00

CHAMPAGNE	Price	Qty required			
Cavalier	37.50	10	375.00		
Britannia	29.50	10		295.00	
Athene	19.50	10			195.00
WINE					
Cavalier	9.75	10	97.50		
Britannia	8.00	10		80.00	
Athene	8.76	10			87.60
COFFEE					
Cavalier	0.75	60	45.00		
Britannia	0.00	60		0.00	
Athene	0.35	60			21.00
WAITERS					
Cavalier	15.00	6	90.00		
Britannia	0.00	0		0.00	
Athene	0.00	0			0.00
BUFFET					
Cavalier	15.00	60	900.00		
Britannia	10.50	60		630.00	
Athene	12.50	60			750.00
TOTALS			2467.50	1610.50	1783.60

Question 3

CHAMPAGNE	Price
Cavalier	37.50
Britannia	29.50
Athene	19.50
WINE	
Cavalier	9.75
Britannia	8.00
Athene	8.76

Question 4

TOTALS	2467.50	1610.50	1783.60
3% Increase	74.03	48.32	53.51

Question 5

Comparative Costs for Wedding (60 guests)

	Cavalier	Britannia	Athene
HALL	500.00	320.00	300.00
CAKE	250.00	150.00	200.00
MC	50.00	0.00	50.00
REST ROOM	60.00	10.50	0.00
PHOTOGRAPHER	100.00	125.00	180.00
TOTAL	960.00	605.50	730.00

CHAMPAGNE	Price	Qty required			
Cavalier	37.50	10	375.00		
Britannia	29.50	10		295.00	
Athene	19.50	10			195.00
WINE					
Cavalier	9.75	10	97.50		
Britannia	8.00	10		80.00	
Athene	8.76	10			87.60
COFFEE					
Cavalier	0.75	60	45.00		
Britannia	0.00	60		0.00	
Athene	0.35	60			21.00
WAITERS					
Cavalier	15.00	6	90.00		
Britannia	0.00	0		0.00	
Athene	0.00	0			0.00
BUFFET					
Cavalier	15.00	60	900.00		
Britannia	10.50	60		630.00	
Athene	12.50	60			750.00
TOTALS			2467.50	1610.50	1783.60
3% Increase			74.03	48.32	53.51
TOTAL COST IF DELAYED			2541.53	1658.82	1837.11

Word Processing Solution

THE OTTERBURN HOTEL GROUP

The Otterburn group is dedicated to providing high-quality accommodation for the discerning traveller at reasonable prices. Our hotels are all luxuriously equipped and are situated in the most desirable positions, both in city centres and the countryside.

The three newest hotels in the group were all opened only last year and maintain the high quality which the public has come to expect from Otterburn.

Britannia Hotel	Lower Cherrington
The Acropolis	Exeter
Royal Edinburgh	Edinburgh

You will be assured of a friendly welcome and excellent food in our restaurants which are an important part of all hotels. An exciting innovation at all our restaurants is the introduction of a full vegetarian menu which is available at all times: for your enjoyment at a family meal, or for a conference or wedding celebration. Details of the hotels in your area are given below.

The bedrooms are all spacious double or twin rooms, including a number of suites, family, non-smoking and Lady Rooms, as well as rooms specifically designed for disabled guests. All have the range of facilities you would expect from hotels of this standard - including remote-controlled television with in-house movies, radio, direct dial telephone, trouser press, hairdryer, beverage tray and the optional 24-hour Room Service.

No doubt you will require a first-class wine to serve at your function, and we give below wine and champagne costs for your information.

1

For couples wishing to book accommodation for the perfect Reception, our facilities are second to none. An idea of the total cost of such an occasion is given below, and we think you will agree that our rates are very competitive.

At the heart of all our hotels lies The Tropicana - a glass-roofed, climate-controlled leisure club. Pools, palm trees, the Coffee Bar and relaxation area, together with the warm climate, create a tropical environment. Whatever the season outside, you can relax and recover from a hectic day's business or sight-seeing by lounging in sub-tropical temperatures.

To complete the scene, our Leisure Club has high-powered sunbeds to provide a fast tan, enabling you to return home looking, as well as feeling, great.

All our hotels boast:

* a fully equipped gymnasium
* sauna
* steamroom
* whirlpool
* cold plunge pool
* swimming pool

and everything is at your disposal, as our guest.

Our fully-trained leisure staff are available to assist and advise at all times.

Graphics Solution

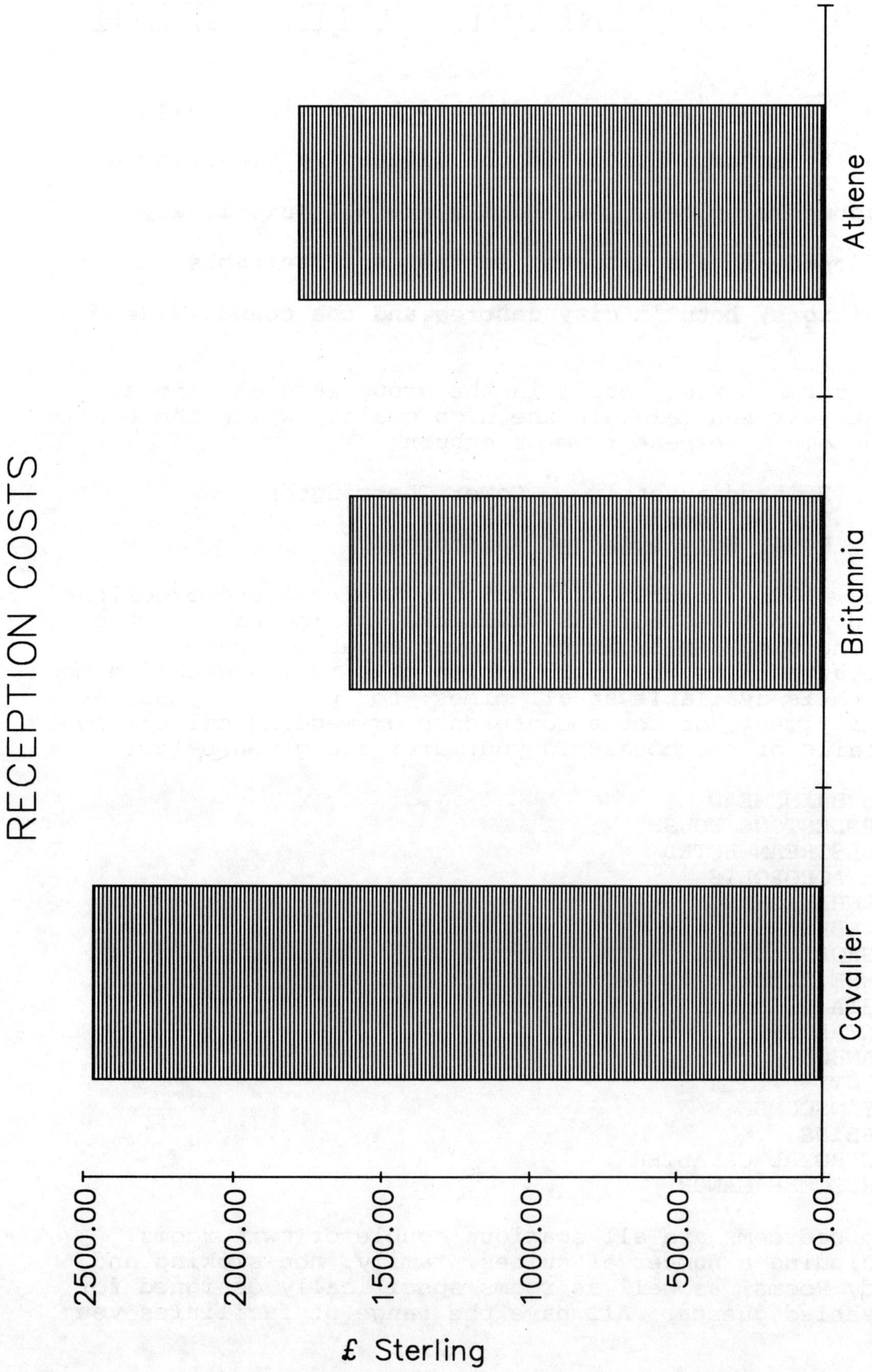

Collating Solution

THE OTTERBURN HOTEL GROUP

The Otterburn group is dedicated to providing high-quality accommodation for the discerning traveller at reasonable prices. Our hotels are all luxuriously equipped and are situated in the most desirable positions, both in city centres and the countryside.

The three newest hotels in the group were all opened only last year and maintain the high quality which the public has come to expect from Otterburn.

Britannia Hotel	Lower Cherrington
The Acropolis	Exeter
Royal Edinburgh	Edinburgh

You will be assured of a friendly welcome and excellent food in our restaurants which are an important part of all hotels. An exciting innovation at all our restaurants is the introduction of a full vegetarian menu which is available at all times: for your enjoyment at a family meal, or for a conference or wedding celebration. Details of the hotels in your area are given below.

THE BRINSMEAD
COPPLESTONE HOUSE
MILLSTREAM HOTEL
THE ACROPOLIS
BURNHAM GRANGE
ST BERNARD'S ABBEY
BISHOP'S LODGE
COMBE HOTEL
RESTAWHILE
CANTALOUPE
IVANHOE
COUNTY
BRYANSCOMBE
ROBBINS
THE ROYAL CAVALIER
LORDCOMBE MANOR

The bedrooms are all spacious double or twin rooms, including a number of suites, family, non-smoking and Lady Rooms, as well as rooms specifically designed for disabled guests. All have the range of facilities you would expect from hotels of this standard - including remote-controlled television with in-house movies, radio, direct dial telephone, trouser press, hairdryer, beverage tray and the optional 24-hour Room Service.

No doubt you will require a first-class wine to serve at your function, and we give below wine and champagne costs for your information.

CHAMPAGNE	Price
Cavalier	37.50
Britannia	29.50
Athene	19.50
WINE	
Cavalier	9.75
Britannia	8.00
Athene	8.76

For couples wishing to book accommodation for the perfect Reception, our facilities are second to none. An idea of the total cost of such an occasion is given below, and we think you will agree that our rates are very competitive.

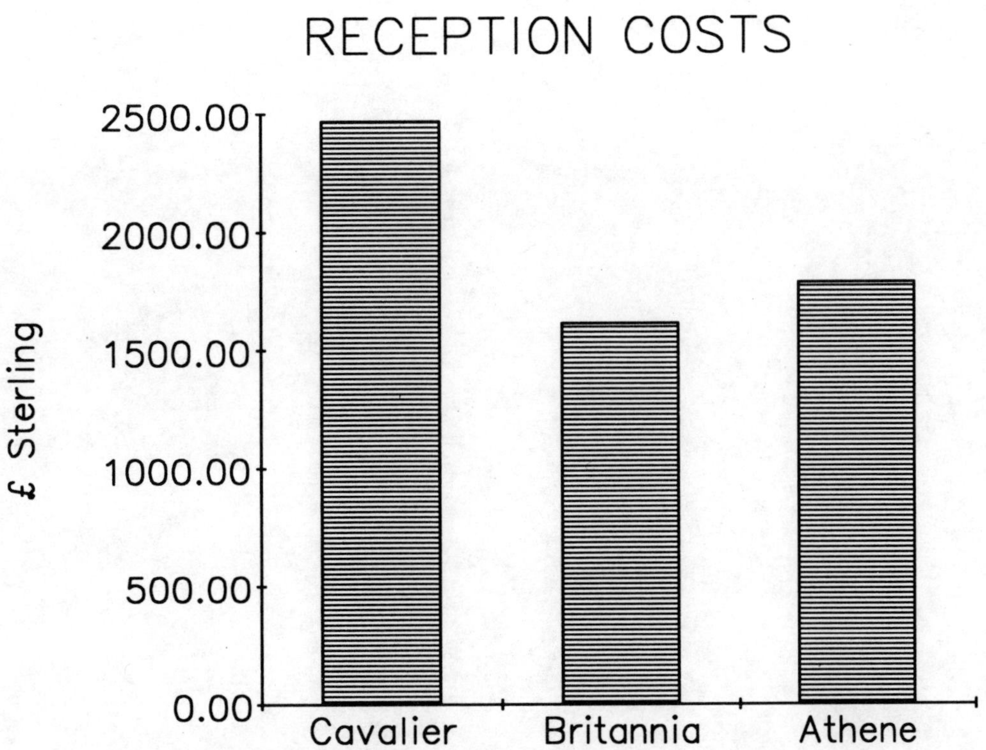

2

At the heart of all our hotels lies The Tropicana - a glass-roofed, climate-controlled leisure club. Pools, palm trees, the Coffee Bar and relaxation area, together with the warm climate, create a tropical environment. Whatever the season outside, you can relax and recover from a hectic day's business or sight-seeing by lounging in sub-tropical temperatures.

To complete the scene, our Leisure Club has high-powered sunbeds to provide a fast tan, enabling you to return home looking, as well as feeling, great.

All our hotels boast:

* a fully equipped gymnasium
* sauna
* steamroom
* whirlpool
* cold plunge pool
* swimming pool

and everything is at your disposal, as our guest.

Our fully-trained leisure staff are available to assist and advise at all times.

3